Library of
Davidson College

ISRAELIS & PALESTINIANS CO-EXISTENCE OR...

THE CREDO OF ELIE ELIACHAR

by PHILIP GILLON

REX COLLINGS, PUBLISHER
London

First published in this edition in Great Britain by Rex Collings Ltd.,
69 Marylebone High Street, London, W.1.

January 1978
ISBN 0860360784

© This book was first published in Israel by Gaalyah Cornfield, Publisher, Tel Aviv in September 1977.

All rights reserved. No part of this publication may be reproduced, stored in a retrieval system, or transmitted, in any form or by any means, electronic, mechanical, photocopying or otherwise, without the prior permission of the publisher.

Designed by Ruth Eilat
Printed in Israel by Ahva Coop. Press, Jerusalem

CONTENTS

Page

CHAPTER 1
A Palestinian Jew Who Believes In Palestinian Arabs 7
A Jew In Palestine — No Starry-Eyed Idealist — Begin's Distortion Of History — The Occupied Areas Are Arab — Palestinians Do Not Deserve Punishment — The Military Threat to Israel — Moderate Arabs

CHAPTER 2
A Prophet In His Own Country 22
Sephardis; Potential Bridges To The Arabs — September, 1973: Experts Agree, War Is Impossible

CHAPTER 3
The Core Of The Problem 27
The Appetite For Land Grows Stronger — Different Schools Of Thought About Palestinian Entity — October, 1973: The Traumatic War — The Jerusalem Dilemma — Let Us Speak To Any Arabs — Eliachar And P.M. Levi Eshkol — We Can Only Survive If We Are Accepted By The Arabs — An Exchange Of Populations Has Occurred — Possibility Of Harmony

CHAPTER 4
Arming Arabs 40
Moderate Arabs Should Defend Themselves — Good News For Arab Moderates — And Jews — A Voice From The Graves Of Arab Palestine

	Page
CHAPTER 5	
One Land, Two Nations	50
The Zionist Predecessor of Herzl, Rabbi Yehuda Alkalay — Early Warning To Zionists — Christian Arab Hatred	
CHAPTER 6	
Mistakes Of The Zionist Leadership	56
Possible Links With Arab Movements — Ussishkin: 'There's No Arab Problem' — Unfamiliarity And Contempt — Socialists Back the Wrong Party — The Ihud	
CHAPTER 7	
Arab Riots And The Peel Commission	74
CHAPTER 8	
Cooperation Through Commerce And Development	81
A Meeting With Emir Abdullah	
CHAPTER 9	
Appeasement In The Palace of St. James	84
The British Trap — The MacDonald Plan	
CHAPTER 10	
The U.N. Commission Of Inquiry	92
Jews Of The Orient	
CHAPTER 11	
Jews In Arab Lands	100
Token Recognition Of Principle	
CHAPTER 12	
They Forget Thee, O Jerusalem	111
CHAPTER 13	
Integration In The Orient	114
After The Sinai Campaign	
CHAPTER 14	
After The Six Day War	118
Moderate Arabs Ignored — Golda Thinks Otherwise	

	Page
CHAPTER 15	
The Smug Years	**128**
Conviction Of Invincibility — Peace From Strength — Demographic Dangers — The Unexpected War	
CHAPTER 16	
The Yom Kippur War	**136**
The Real Culprit — Illusions Never Die — Israel Must Recognize The Palestinians — Zionism's Original Misconception — A Semitic People In A Middle Eastern Land — The Sons Of Shem	
CHAPTER 17	
Arafat At The U.N.	**147**
Arafat's Intransigence — Announce Recognition	
CHAPTER 18	
The Lebanese Agony	**152**
The Shock of 1958 — Syrian Aims — False Solution	
CHAPTER 19	
Begin Comes To Power	**161**
The Honeymoon With Carter — American Interests — Israel's Military Might — The De Gaulle Precedent	
EPILOGUE	
Co-Existence In Separate States	**171**
The Arab Attitude	

FOREWORD

This book is based on chapters from a book in Hebrew, "Living With Palestinians," by Elie Eliachar, published in 1975, augmented by numerous discussions I have had with him since. The translation from Hebrew is by Tsippora Raphael.

PHILIP GILLON

Jerusalem
September, 1977

CHAPTER ONE

A PALESTINIAN JEW WHO BELIEVES IN PALESTINIAN ARABS

Who are the Palestinian Arabs? Do they constitute a separate people entitled to their own homeland and the right of self-determination? Can they be represented by the Palestine Liberation Organisation, the body formed by various groups using weapons of terror and sabotage against Israel? Can Israel be compelled by international pressure to surrender the West Bank area and Gaza, of former Palestine, occupied by her during the Six Day War? Is she obliged to hold this region, which constituted the Biblical kingdoms of Judea and Samaria (Israel) to fulfil some Divine Will? On finding the correct answers to these questions depends not only the future of the Middle East, but that of the entire world.

The election of Menahem Begin as prime minister of Israel brought to power a leader committed to the doctrine that Israel could never withdraw from Judea and Samaria, not only because of security considerations, but because of a complex of mystic and nationalistic considerations. While he announced that he wanted to negotiate with leaders of Arab states without any pre-conditions, he insisted that he would never talk to any members of the Palestine Liberation Organisation, whom he denounced as murderers. He repeated the doctrine of his predecessors like Golda Meir and Yitzhak Rabin — Israel could never agree to the creation of a Palestinian Arab state between the Jordan River and Israel's eastern frontier.

But Menahem Begin was not the only leader in the world to assume power in 1977. Thousands of miles away, Jimmy Carter was sworn in as president of the U.S.A., the country committed by a long tradition to support Israel. Without America's massive military and financial aid, Israel could not have survived.

President Jimmy Carter produced a completely new set of answers to the key Middle East questions. The Palestinian Arabs, he said, do constitute a separate nation entitled to a homeland in the West Bank and the Gaza Strip, as soon as they recognise Israel's right to exist within secure and recognised borders. Carter demanded that Israel should withdraw from the West Bank according to a time-table ensuring her security; he drew a distinction between her security borders and her political borders.

His views were supported by the nine countries forming the European Common Community, and, of course, by the Arabs, Russians and most of the Third World. As a result of the changes the new President brought into American thinking, or at least into published American thinking, Israel was put in grave danger of standing virtually alone in the world. Nevertheless, to be out of step with the majority does not necessarily mean that one is wrong. Begin recalled the world-wide acclaim for the Chamberlain-Daladier agreement at Munich to dismember Czechoslovakia so as to appease Hitler; most people had happily acclaimed a move said to have brought peace to the world for twenty years.

A Jew in Palestine

No man in the world is better qualified to discuss the existence or non-existence of the Palestinian Arabs as a separate people than Elie Eliachar. He grew up among such Arabs; he is one of the few Jews in Israel who knows large numbers of Arabs intimately. Not only was he himself born in Jerusalem, but so were his forefathers: in the dedication of his book in Hebrew, 'On Living With The Palestinians', to his grandchildren, he notes proudly that they will be the eighteenth generation of the family to live in Israel. He writes in his dedication that 18 is a lucky number for Jews — letters of the Hebrew alphabet are used to write numbers in Hebrew, and the letters which stand for the number 18 also spell out the word 'life'. He believes that life for his grandchildren depends on finding the way to peace with the Arabs.

Members of the Eliachar family were prominent for generations in all aspects of Jewish life in what was then Palestine. Chief Rabbis, rabbis, businessmen, communal leaders — large numbers of them were Eliachars. His great grandfather and his grandfather were the Chief Rabbis of Palestine — "First in Zion". His maternal grandfather, Joseph Bey Navon, was responsible for building the railroad from Jerusalem to Jaffa. The Eliachar House, close to the Western Wall, was the linch-pin of the famous complex of Jewish synagogues in the Old City of Jerusalem, restored thanks to him after the Six-Day War.

Elie's father, Yitzhak Shemaya Eliachar, a very well-known business and communal leader, was appointed deputy mayor of Jerusalem by the British in 1917, a week after General Allenby took the city. He was the first Jew to hold such an appointment in the modern era.

Later Elie himself became an elected deputy mayor of Jerusalem. In his youth he studied medicine in Beirut, and law in Cairo and Jerusalem; during World War I, he served side by side with many leading Arabs as an officer in the Turkish Army. When the British took over Palestine, he became a member of the Mandatory Administration, and was placed in charge of trade and industry, serving as well as Official Receiver. His service in these posts strengthened his many contacts with Arabs.

He became a leading industrialist in Palestine, later in Israel. Prior to the creation of the state, he was one of the 11 members of the Supreme Council of the Haganah, the underground Jewish self-defence organisation, which preceded the Israel Defence Forces, under Ben-Gurion's chairmanship. He was President of the Kehila in Jerusalem and a member of the Jewish National Assembly prior to 1948. After the state was formed, he served for several years in the Knesset.

A man with such a record might be expected to be a firm supporter of the Establishment. But Elie Eliachar supported two unpopular causes which put him at odds with those in power — the Palestinian Arabs and the Jews from Oriental lands, who had immigrated to Israel since 1948, and whom he once described in the Knesset as 'the second Israel' — a description still apt to this day.

Leading Arabs were frequent visitors to the Eliachar home when Elie was a boy. In his business activities, he had numerous dealings with Arabs.

He told me once, 'I had deals with Arabs involving hundreds of thousands of pounds, without a single receipt or piece of paper changing hands, and without the intervention of lawyers being needed. Yet I have never known an Arab to break his word or to try to cheat me. It is absurd to assume, as so many Jewish leaders do, that Arabs cannot be trusted'.

These dealings were not confined to money matters, but to all kinds of arrangements. For example, when he helped to set up the first Jewish airline in Palestine in the 'thirties, he had prolonged negotiations with Misr Airways about landing rights in Egypt and Lebanon. The project was a very complicated one. Once he and his Arab counterparts had reached a verbal agreement, everything ran without the slightest hitch or argument, although it took many months for the lawyers and accountants to reduce the transaction to formal documents.

After Israel took over the West Bank in 1967, former Arab friends, cut off from Israel for 19 years, resumed dealings with Eliachar's office, still on a basis of mutual trust. Many of the Arabs came to his home to renew their deep friendships with him and his wife.

He maintains that one of the tragedies of Israel is that Jewish leaders, coming from Europe, knew nothing about the Arabs, and made little effort to remedy this ignorance. 'They were determined to establish in Israel the same sort of society in which they had lived in Eastern and Central Europe, a closed Jewish society', he says. 'They accepted the European tradition of despising the Levant, the assumption that "levantinism" is a term of contempt. Yet here was the paradox: the Jews wanted to live in the Levant, to be accepted as part of it by the Arabs.

'Thus the early leaders of the Zionist Movement tried to create in Palestine a sort of island, on which they hoped to isolate themselves from the ocean of human beings around them. This isolationism exists even today. We hardly ever teach the Arabic language, or Arab history, or Arab geography in our schools.'

No Starry-Eyed Idealist
It would be a gross error to dismiss Eliachar as a starry-eyed idealist, in love with some romantic concept of the noble Arabs, who are incapable of ill-treating Jews. During the 'forties and early 'fifties, Eliachar knew better perhaps than any other man how much the Jews of the Orient suffered in terrible pogroms inspired by Arab governments. Eliachar fought a long and successful campaign to extricate these Jews and to bring them to Israel. He knows that Israel must always be strong enough to defend herself. But her own need for security must not blind her, according to him, to the legitimate aspirations of the Palestinian Arabs.

With this background, Elie Eliachar certainly knows the Palestinian Arabs in a way that Menahem Begin, Golda Meir and Yitzhak Rabin never got to know them. And he has no doubt that they constitute a separate nation different from the other Arabs in the Middle East. He disputes a claim made by Golda Meir and others that the Palestinian Arabs are a fiction, a post-1967 invention; on the contrary, he believes that they were the core of the Middle East problem from 1920 onwards.

Begin's Distortion of History
About Menahem Begin's attitude to the West Bank, Eliachar says, 'Begin is introducing a new concept into modern world politics — instead of claiming the

right to hold the occupied areas indefinitely for security reasons, as his predecessors did, he is now staking in addition a mystic-religious-chauvinistic claim to the West Bank. Thus the Likud and its supporters, Gush Emunim, allege that "the whole of Eretz Yisrael" was granted to the Jews by Divine Power, and that it is the duty of the Jews to retain this region, by force of arms if necessary, thus subjugating over a million and a half Arabs.

'No person of goodwill can tolerate with a clean conscience this expansionism under the pretence of fulfilling God's will, an assertion that to decent men, Jew and non-Jew alike, smacks of taking the name of God in vain.

'There is no justification whatsover in the Bible or in history for saying that Israel's eastern border has been ordained by God to be the Jordan River, or that the borders attained as a result of the conquests in the Six Day War are fixed by divine precepts. At no stage in the history of The Land did the borders of any state dominated by the Jews coincide exactly with the contiguous borders of post-1967 Israel, including the occupied areas.

'At the time of David and Solomon, their sovereignty was accepted by all the smaller city states that existed in the Israel of their times, extending up to Damascus. But the Mediterranean coast was held by the Phoenicians or Sidonians, the Philistines, and others, whom Saul fought unsuccessfully, and with whom David established cordial relations, made even stronger by Solomon.

'Admittedly, the divine promise to Abraham mentioned an area extending from the Euphrates River to the Nile River. But to suggest that this vast region should become the modern land of Israel goes beyond even the wildest and most extravagant claims of Begin and his supporters, or the dreams of Jewish mystics.

'In fact, the great Jewish mystics contemplated redemption through the Messiah coming to Jerusalem, not through military conquest and occupation by force of areas inhabited by vast numbers of non-Jews.

'Let me remind those who rely on the Scriptures to justify refusal to give back an inch of the West Bank that the Almighty, through the prophecies of Isaiah, foretold the establishment of good relations with our neighbours: "In that Day shall Israel be the third with Egypt and Assyria, even a blessing in the midst of The Land" (19-24). Thus the Bible urges us to strive for peace, not for conquest and occupation against the will of the inhabitants.

'The great English scholar, the Rev. Dr. James Parkes, a lifelong friend of the Jews, wrote in his book, "Whose Land?": "In all the 3,500 years of its recorded history, the Land of Israel has never been exclusively the house of a single people. Even when the Children of Israel regarded it as their promised land, they very quickly grew out of the idea that they would be the exclusive dwellers in it. They started indeed by proclaiming that their God called upon them to destroy Amalek and the other previous inhabitants. But they abandoned the idea more than 2,500 years ago...".'

Elie Eliachar knows that many Israelis will attack him for quoting a non-Jew, however renowned as a scholar, on an issue which they consider to be exclusively Jewish.

He says, 'Dr. Parkes is a renowned scholar of Jewish history. Historical facts cannot be denied or dis-

Jacob Shaul Eliachar, Chief Rabbi of Palestine 'First in Zion,' great-grandfather of Elie Eliachar. He insisted in 1870 that Arabic should be taught in Jewish schools

Joseph Bey Navon, builder of the railroad from Jaffa to Jerusalem, maternal grandfather of Elie Eliachar

torted to justify conquest. And I must add that I acquired my views in my early schooldays, from talks with great rabbis and secular teachers, and extensive readings.

'I have absolute faith in the Jewish past and the Jewish destiny. I come from a Zionist family and I have been a Zionist by conviction, elected to many Zionist Congresses, ever since the 14th Congress held in Vienna in 1925. I believe passionately and absolutely in our Jewish right to our own historic national Homeland — in the Land — the Land of Israel — but not in what Begin and his supporters consider to be the Entire Land, within the post-1967 borders.

'Jerusalem is of course the heart of the dream of the Return. Ever since David moved his capital to Uru-Shalim, the City of Peace, and Solomon built the first Temple there, the City acquired its sanctity for the Jews. Since the destruction of the Second Temple and the Dispersion of the Jews, Jerusalem became the symbol of our Faith, the vital spiritual element for the survival of the Jewish People. The same cannot be said about Judea and Samaria, which split Jewish unity and sovereignty after Solomon.

'As for Gaza, it was not always Jewish. We need only recall what Samson did to the people of Gaza and what Delilah and the Philistines did to him.'

The Occupied Areas are Arab
'These areas are inhabited by hundreds of thousands of Arabs. Despite a vast investment of treasure and effort, in the years that have passed since the occupation began in 1967, only a few thousand Jews have settled there. Behind all the ballyhoo about new settle-

ments in the West Bank and the Gaza Strip, the truth is that settlements established there are really little more than military garrisons, occupied temporarily by young people doing their military service.

'When those people who claim that Israel must hold the entire West Bank cannot find any authority in the Bible for their assertions, they shift their argument to rely on modern history. They point out that both the Balfour Declaration and the League of Nations Mandate contemplated originally that the Jewish National Home should include the whole of Palestine as it existed in 1917 as a Turkish province, that Transjordan was subsequently taken away by Winston Churchill and given to Emir Abdullah. So, they argue, they are settling for less than the world promised the Jews after World War I, if they say they only want the Land up to the Jordan River, and magnanimously allow the state of Jordan to exist unchallenged.

'But the truth is that Zionism did not claim at any time the right to oust the Arabs from their native country, or to deny them their national rights, which were specifically protected under the Declaration and the Mandate. Dr. Chaim Weizmann, the President of the World Zionist Organisation, repeatedly re-affirmed this principle. In an article he published in the "Palestine Post" on September 16, 1936, he described Palestine as "a common Fatherland for Arab and Jew". In 1937, the Jews accepted the principle of Palestine, without Transjordan, being divided into two states, one Jewish and one for the Palestinian Arabs, when they approved the recommendations in principle of the Peel Commission. Nobody bothered then about the Divine Will. It was the Arabs who rejected the Peel concept. Again in 1947, when the United Nations voted for the creation of a Jewish state and an Arab state, the Jews accepted the proposal with jubilation, they danced with joy in the streets. We did not say then that there is no such people as the Palestinian Arabs.

'In their folly, the Arabs rejected all international proposals, and tried by war to prevent the creation and survival of the Jewish state. They failed to achieve these objectives despite riots, terrorism and five wars. But no international agreement or document of any kind ever guaranteed to Israel the right to retain land acquired by military conquests, even in wars fought to defend herself. On the contrary, by accepting resolutions 242 and 338, we endorsed the principle that no state can retain lands occupied in battles.

'Underlying some Israeli thinking is belief in the old principles, "Woe to the victim", and "To the victor, the spoils." The argument is that the Arabs, after vast tracts of land were occupied by Israel during wars the Arabs started, cannot come forward, like losers in a football match, and say, "We apologise for going to war. Now give us back our lands, and let us go back to the *status quo ante bellum*." Israelis relying on the old doctrine of might is right point to the manner in which the U.S.S.R. has dominated countries occupied by it during World War II. But nobody believes that the Russian policy is morally justified. From a practical point of view, also, for a tiny country like Israel to imagine that it can behave like mighty Russia is like the frog that believed it could behave like a bull.

'Holding land against the will of the inhabitants, subjugating over a million and a half people, is completely alien to every principle of liberty and self-determination that Jews have traditionally held dear, the very principles that provide the moral basis for Zionism.'

Palestinians Do Not Deserve Punishment
'It cannot even be said that the Palestinian Arabs deserve to be "punished" for going to war. In fact, the wars were not waged by them, but by sovereign states like Egypt, Syria and Jordan, which set out officially to "rescue them". Jordan and Egypt administered the West Bank and the Gaza Strip, respectively, between 1948 and 1967, for their own aggrandisement, not to give self-determination to the Palestinian Arabs.

'The Bible, history, Zionism, morality — none of these support the claims of Begin and the Gush Emunim that Israel is obliged by some higher force to keep the West Bank. Practical politics makes such retention, in defiance of America and the entire world, impossible.

'Ever since 1920, the Palestinian Arabs have asserted their right to a homeland. They must be given one. The obvious place is the West Bank, combined with the Gaza Strip. There they can decide for themselves if they want some kind of federation with Jordan, or Syria, or, in time — I hope — with Israel. Obviously, too, the setting up of a Palestinian Arab state must be combined with absolute guarantees of Israel's security; it must be effected in such a way that Israel is not imperilled. This will be very difficult, but it is not impossible.

'The alternative is to precipitate another war, perhaps one in which the entire Middle East will go up in flames. Terrible catastrophes will follow inevitably, such as a complete oil boycott or even the destruction of the oilfields. Some Israelis are even prepared to contemplate the use of atomic weapons as an alternative to surrendering the West Bank. Like Samson, they are prepared to bring down the Temple and to die with the Philistines. This seems to be the approach of the P.L.O. too!'

The Military Threat to Israel
'Begin says that it would be impossible to set up a Palestinian Arab state on the West Bank because they would be able to use artillery against Israel's heavily populated areas, only a few miles away. When the Syrian dictator Shishakli threatened to attack Tel-Aviv, only 600 kilometres from Damascus and 30 minutes flying time, Ben-Gurion reminded him calmly that Damascus was just as near to Tel-Aviv and the Israeli planes could fly faster.

'Until real peace is established, Israel will have to maintain very strong defence forces, constantly on the alert. Eternal vigilance is the price we have to pay for living in a small land surrounded by neighbours who are at present hostile. Until we have overcome that hostility by getting real peace in the area, we must be ready all the time to deter or defeat any attacks. On a vast scale, the U.S.A. also maintains unceasing vigilance.

'Of course, creating a Palestinian state on the West Bank and in the Gaza Strip involves risks. Not creating it, but trying to retain the areas in defiance of the entire world, does not involve a risk — it involves a certainty, the certainty that there will be another war. It requires great courage to take risks that may bring dangers — or peace. It is an act of despair to choose the path of blood, destruction and death.

'There is still the question of with whom we are to negotiate. It would certainly have been better if we had negotiated in 1967 and 1968 with moderate Palestinian Arab leaders, living on the West Bank and Gaza, who were prepared then to talk to us. Moshe Dayan, then Minister of Defence in control of the occupied areas, refused to countenance any such negotiations, or any political activity by these moderate Palestinian Arabs, or any recognition of them as national leaders in the political sense. He only allowed them to engage in municipal politics and activities. His attitudes were endorsed by Golda Meir's Government. The vacuum thus created was filled by the Palestine Liberation Organisation. This is a great pity, but it is a fact.

'Now we must come to terms with the facts we helped to create. The Palestine Liberation Organisation has been recognised by all the Arab states, and by most countries in the world, as the representatives of the Palestinian Arabs. If they agree to recognize Israel's right to exist in safe and recognized borders, how can we refuse to talk to them? Former terrorists everywhere have become respected political leaders. It is better to talk to them than to talk only to ourselves.

'My dreams, my hopes, my expectations for Israel and Zionism are that our leaders will see the light and will negotiate a basis for us to live at peace with the Palestinian Arabs. We must revert to our source — *we must return to the East as Easterners* — seeking coexistence and collaboration with the Arabs around us. We have so very much in common; our religions,

Judaism and Islam; our languages, Hebrew and Arabic; our descent from Abraham. We must fit into the pattern of the Middle East, while retaining and expanding the best of the West.'

Moderate Arabs
'There are moderates in the Arab world, like the wise King Hassan of Morocco. In the presence of President Anwar El-Sadat of Egypt he declared in July, 1977, "Jews and Arabs are being challenged, historically, to combine efforts for the revival of the glory of the Middle East, as descendants of Abraham."

'Why must we assume that Hussein, Sadat and Hassan do not mean what they say? Let us accept the challenge. I believe that it can be done, the miracle of peace can be achieved, in accordance with our daily prayers... "with enduring strength and peace!"'

CHAPTER TWO

A PROPHET IN HIS OWN COUNTRY

Nowhere in the Bible is there any indication that Jeremiah's comments on the national policies were received with enthusiasm by the people; it is an exasperating trait in a prophet to be right, especially when his prophecies are pessimistic. Elie Eliachar has found himself all too often in the position of being able to say, 'I told you so' to his fellow-Israelis, a position which has not contributed to his popularity. Yet he is really not a pessimist; he is convinced that it is possible to solve the Arab-Jewish problem in the Middle East, if only both sides would have the courage to lay down their swords.

In fairness to other leading Zionists, it must be conceded that not everybody can make personal contacts with the same ease as Eliachar. He is a man who establishes friendships with other people, Jews and Moslems and Christians alike. In his philosophy, seeing other people as clichés and stereotypes instead of as human beings is a poor basis for shaping a sound political policy. He claims that Zionist leaders, with their European colonisers' arrogance and contempt for the Levantines, the 'natives,' developed an attitude of over-confidence that resulted in the nearly fatal complacency, which culminated in the tragic errors of the Yom Kippur War in October, 1973.

This European view that the Levant was to be despised also affected the approach of the European Jews to their fellow-Jews, the so-called *Sephardim*.

'There was admittedly a difference in the types of Jewish societies that existed in Europe and the Orient at the beginning of the twentieth century', Eliachar concedes. 'The Enlightenment, which penetrated the ghettos after the Napoleonic Wars, did not reach into the *harahs* and *mellahs* (ghettos), as the areas in which many Oriental Jews lived were known. The Sephardi Jews were surrounded by Arab societies, that were rigid, feudal, dictatorial. They were all subjects of the Turkish sultan, and the Ottoman Empire was despotic and reactionary. It is true that Jews reached positions of importance, serving as ministers of state since the Middle Ages. But the Sephardi communities were bypassed by the winds of change that swept across Europe in the latter half of the nineteenth century, and the first half of the twentieth.'

Sephardis — Potential Bridges to the Arabs

'The difference in backgrounds was no excuse for the neglect of the Sephardi Jews by the leaders of the Zionist Movement and the State of Israel. Paradoxically, although furthest from the corridors of power, they were — and are — the best qualified to understand the Arabs. Unfortunately, the bridge to the Arabs they could have provided was never used.'

These two long struggles — for better understanding with the Arabs and better treatment for the Sephardi Jews — have dominated Elie Eliachar's life. He has found that both themes have been unpopular, because both ran counter to the main currents in Israel.

Some Jews branded him a defeatist for insisting that something had to be done about the Palestinians; others ridiculed his admonitions and called him a prophet of doom. When the catastrophes he forecast took place, his unpopularity increased.

The criticism intensified when he became the Honorary President of the Council for Peace with the Palestinians, formed in 1975 by a group of famous Israelis, including a general, a hero of the illegal immigration days, a former Director-General of the Treasury, several prominent intellectuals and politicians. They had the temerity to join Eliachar in suggesting that Israel should talk to the Palestinians, even to the P.L.O.

A member of the Labour Alignment denounced the Council in the Knesset, and demanded that its members should be charged as criminals.

There are still surprisingly few Israelis who realise that the solution to the problem of the Palestinians does not lie in Israel's military prowess alone. Prior to the Yom Kippur War in October, 1973, this delusion of grandeur was very widespread. Eliachar's voice was indeed one crying in the wilderness during the period between 1967 and 1973, when he tried to warn the country of the folly of assuming that the Arabs would come abjectly to heel, and would make peace on terms dictated by Israel.

On August 18, 1973, Eliachar submitted an article to 'Ha'aretz,' Israel's leading morning newspaper, which he called 'Not By the Sword Alone'. In it he warned that Israel's belief in her military invincibility rested on shaky ground, and that Israel's insistence on retaining the territories occupied in 1967 would make the Arabs so desperate that they might try another war. Even if Israel won, he wrote, the losses on both sides would be great. He called for 'a change of attitude, a new approach, a genuine wish for peace'.

September, 1973 — Experts Agree War Is Impossible
The article was returned to Eliachar, unpublished, in September, 1973. 'Ha'aretz' explained that leading Arabists and military experts in Israel all agreed that war was impossible. A month later, on October 6, Egypt and Syria attacked, and caught the Israel Defence Forces completely unprepared.

Although Israel managed to recover from the first terrible setbacks on the battlefields in the Sinai Desert and the Golan Heights, the overall outcome of the Yom Kippur War was just as disastrous as Eliachar had warned. The Arabs proved that they could fight with the sophisticated weapons provided by the Russians; even worse, from the Israeli point of view, they developed the mighty weapon of the oil boycott, which affected the economies of the entire Western world, and turned many countries against Israel.

Israeli leaders had always ignored the power of oil. In 1969, Eliachar wrote an article, a copy of which he sent to Moshe Dayan, then Minister of Defence, in which he pointed out that the world was becoming entirely dependent on Arab oil, and that an oil boycott would bring the West to its knees. Dayan rejected the warning out of hand. Time and again he and Golda Meir, the Prime Minister during this critical period, ridiculed all talk of an oil boycott, saying, 'If the Arabs don't want to sell their oil, let them drink it.' Even in 1973, shortly before the boycott proved so effective, they were still bandying this witty thought around.

After the Yom Kippur War, Dayan said in an interview, 'Who could have foreseen the power of oil in politics before the embargo?' Dayan also minimised the danger of Russian intervention in the Middle East.

Many similar warnings failed to stir leaders and public, who preferred their illusions to facing the truth. Being right so often in the past is some indication that Eliachar may be right also about the present and the future. He is still passionately determined to make both Jews and Arabs realise that they must abandon forever the folly of war and the empty hope that either people can dictate its will on the other. 'The way of the sword is as hopeless for one side as for the other: there can be no true victories for either Jew or Arab, only mock glories that are misleading and ephemeral,' he says. 'The one true road to security is the road of peace.'

Eliachar says, 'I am an old man now — 79 — and I have had my full share of honours and success and happiness. Now I have to prepare for the last station in life. But more than ever I feel it my duty to strive to make both Jews and Arabs seek true understanding of each other, so that our children and our children's children will not know the miseries of conflict that we have had to endure. Call it "Shalom" or call it "Soulh" — we all have the same goal — PEACE!'

CHAPTER THREE

THE CORE OF THE PROBLEM

Most Israeli leaders took it for granted that the Six Day War would bring an end to the long agony of the Arab-Jewish conflict, but they assumed that the end would be on terms proposed by the Israeli Government. Key members of the Cabinet, like Golda Meir, Moshe Dayan and Abba Eban announced to the world that no such national entity as the Palestinians ever existed, and that it was absurd to contemplate the creation of yet another Arab state to satisfy Palestinian nationalist aspirations.

The first reaction after the Six Day War was to hold the areas occupied during the War only as bargaining counters; with some exceptions, like Jerusalem, the Golan Heights and Sharm el-Sheikh, the rest of the territories were to be traded back to Jordan, Egypt and Syria for the peace expected to come after the armistice. Then the Arab Summit Conference at Khartoum passed its famous four-noes resolution — no peace, no recognition of Israel, no negotiations, and insistence on the rights of the Palestinian Arabs to return to their homes — and it became apparent that Israel was in for a long haul.

The Appetite for Land Grows Stronger
This meant that the occupation of the conquered territories would continue indefinitely. The original argu-

ment for refusal to return the territories was that their retention was essential for Israel's security. As time passed, what had begun as a plan to hold land as bargaining counters was gradually transformed into a desire to hold land for its own sake. The appetite grew with what it fed upon. Historical and religious reasons were found, quite apart from security, to justify creating a 'greater Israel,' stretching from the Jordan River to the Mediterranean, and from the Golan Heights to south of El Arish.

There were some who opposed the trend. Among them was David Ben-Gurion, who, addressing the Knesset on the occasion of Israel's 20th anniversary, declared: 'For the sake of peace I would gladly surrender all the areas occupied during the Six Day War, with the exception of Jerusalem... Later, in conversation with Eliachar, he added: 'Jerusalem and the Golan Heights would be subject to arduous negotiations for a compromise.' But Ben-Gurion's former disciples, who had taken over the seats of the mighty in Israel, rejected the Old Man's wise views.

If Ben-Gurion could make no impact on Israeli complacency and dreams of expansion, what chance did Eliachar have with his Jeremiads? Eliachar was horrified, for example, by an interview which Prime Minister Golda Meir gave to Frank Giles of the 'Sunday Times' of London, in which she said:

'There is no such thing as a Palestinian nation. When was there an independent Palestinian people with a Palestine State? It was either southern Syria before the First World War, and then it was Palestine, including Jordan. It was not as though there was a Palestinian entity in Palestine considering itself a Palestinian people, and we came and threw them out, and took their country away from them. They did not exist.'

Turning to the subject of Palestinian statehood, Mrs. Meir said that she did not favour the setting up of such a state. 'There are,' she claimed, 'fourteen Arab states with immense territories, with natural resources. What would this tiny state of the West Bank really mean as to its viability, as to its possibility of existence?'

Statements like these, Eliachar believes, did Israel great harm in the eyes of the world at large, among the Arabs, and even among the Jews outside Israel. Israel was seen as an arrogant conqueror, determined to hold what she had won in war. On the other side, extremists became more and more dominant among the Palestinians, in reaction to the Israeli attitude. But Israeli military experts were bemused by their easy victory in 1967. Instead of realising that only peace could bring security, they relied on 'secure borders' and 'invincible lines.' The Bar-Lev line and the Golan Heights created a Maginot Line complex. On the eve of the Yom Kippur War, some thirty famous Israeli Orientalists joined with Dayan in declaring that there could be no war for ten years, because Israel enjoyed a technical advantage of at least seven to one when considering the individual soldiers, an even higher advantage when the military component was considered as a whole.

Different Schools of Thought About Palestinian Entity
Eliachar notes sardonically that there were several different schools of thought among the experts to

justify the refusal to come to terms with the reality of the existence of a Palestinian entity.

One group argued that the creation of a Palestinian state on the West Bank and in the Gaza Strip would amount to no more than setting up an Israeli 'protectorate' in the disgraced colonial tradition. Another school argued that the establishment of such a Palestinian state would expose Israel to renewed attacks by regular Arab armies and terrorist organisations from a few kilometres across the border. A third group objected that recognition of a Palestinian national entity would be only a first concession: this state would then demand a return to the boundaries recommended in the United Nations Partition Resolution of 1947.

While finding these widely differing reasons for rejecting the case for a Palestinian entity, its opponents were unanimous in condemning those who advocated recognizing the realities of its existence as 'defeatists,' misled 'bleeding heart liberals,' and even out and out communists.

October, 1973: The Traumatic War

Then came the Yom Kippur War, completely confounding all the theories of the 'hawks,' including the claim that the Bar-Lev Suez Canal line and the Golan Heights line were invincible. The Arabs crossed these lines with ease. It might be thought that the bankruptcy of the hawkish policy would bring about a complete change of thinking in Israel. Unfortunately, the tragic losses in dead and wounded, the sights on television screens of Israeli soldiers subjected to the humiliation of captivity, the proof by Arab soldiers

Yitzhak Shemaya Eliachar, Deputy Mayor of Jerusalem, appointed in 1917, father of Elie Eliachar

Dr. Chaim Weizmann with Lord Samuel, 1951

Dr. Chaim Weizmann and Emir Feisal at Ma'an, Jordan, 1918. As a result of Weizmann's negotiations with Feisal, the Emir wrote a letter to Judge Felix Frankfurter in which he approved of Zionism. Weizmann wrote in an article in 1936, 'Palestine is a common Fatherland for Arab and Jew'

that they could also fight, the efficiency of the Russian weapons in their hands, and the world-wide triumph of the Arab oil boycott caused such a trauma among Israelis that they still would not accept Eliachar's home truths. The fact that he had been proved right seemed only to exasperate the people. They preferred to try to brush the nightmare of October, 1973 under the carpet, to pretend that everything was as it had been in the halcyon years between June 1967 and September, 1973. They went even further: they persuaded themselves that it was only the fault of Dr. Kissinger or the U.N. or somebody else that they had not destroyed the Arab armies completely.

Only a small minority acknowledged that military victories could never resolve the Middle East crisis. There were still more hawks than doves in the aviary. Elie Eliachar went on pouring out articles, trying in vain to compel the nation to face the realities of life in the Middle East.

'Why,' he demanded in a typical article he wrote in 1974, 'do our leaders persist in their opposition to setting up a Palestinian state, which, in time, may join Israel in a sort of federal arrangement? All the blueprints and plans now being submitted by Israel's various political parties and groups have so far failed to take cognizance of the elementary fact that, no matter what happens, the Arabs of the West Bank and the Gaza Strip are bound to remain in our midst or in our region. If we keep opposing their right to self-determination and to national independence, it is likely that they will eventually join forces with the Arabs of Israel, endangering our existence from within.'

Black Tuesday, 1976

It is worth noting that this prediction that Israeli Arabs, whom the Jews called 'our Arabs,' would join the Arabs outside Israel was written before Black Tuesday, March 30, 1976, the day on which Israeli Arabs in Galilee rioted because of the proposed expropriation of Arabs' lands. The Government tactlessly explained that its aim was, 'to Judaize the Galilee,' a part of Israel in which Israeli Arabs constitute a majority. During the riots, the Arabs screamed pro-P.L.O., Palestine nationalist sentiments. Israeli Jews were horrified by the discovery that many of their 'own' Arabs did not love them, and were not satisfied with being a minority in a Jewish state.

Eliachar went on in his article: 'Nor should we forget the demographic aspects of the problem, namely, that the Palestinian Arabs have a very high birthrate. A new wave of Jewish mass immigration does not seem to be at hand.

The Jerusalem Dilemma

'But does the present Palestinian leadership really want to talk to us? And need we help to set up another Arab state when so many such states exist and fight us in the United Nations and other international forums? What would happen in Jordan if the Palestinians were to decide to set up their own state? And, finally, how is Israel to be persuaded to accept the kind of Jewish-Arab "condominium" I suggest for Jerusalem?

'To the first question, whether the Palestinians are willing to talk to us, I would unhesitatingly assert that there does exist the possibility to conduct such talks.

At any rate, why not put the matter to the test? We should test also whether we are willing to meet and talk on an equal footing with the Palestinians in an attempt to find ways for attaining true and lasting peace. If the tests fail, nothing will have been lost or changed, but we will have proved that we are seeking peace — and this will be appreciated by world public opinion far more than proclamations unsupported by action.

'As to the fear of still another Arab state being added to those already in existence, which oppose Israel, one more Arab state will make no difference. By extending recognition to a Palestinian Arab state, we would only be acknowledging what is fast becoming a fact — the Palestinians have become an important factor in the international arena. Agreeing to be a party to the setting up of a Palestinian state would bring us nearer to peace with the Arabs in the territories under our administration, and through them, with the rest of the Palestinians and with the Arab world as a whole.

Let Us Speak to Any Arabs
'About 1,300,000 Palestinians live in our midst today. Most of them want a peaceful settlement with us. Although no serious movement towards revolt has emerged among them so far, this must not be regarded as a permanent state of affairs. We must take the initiative so as to come to an arrangement with them. It is saddening to hear Israeli leaders declare that there is nobody amongst the Palestinians with whom we can talk. "Are we to talk to Arafat?" they ask. My answer is: Why not? — provided Arafat can

show that he speaks for the Palestinians and that he declares that Israel exists as of right. Quite a few of yesterday's "terrorists" have become respected leaders in their independent countries. This has happened in Israel itself.

'We should encourage any group of Palestinians that represents the Palestinian people and speak in its name. I know that many Israeli leaders argue that they never missed a single opportunity to establish contact with Arabs, including Palestinians, so as to reach a peaceful settlement.

'This is not altogether true. The policy in the occupied West Bank and Gaza areas, ever since 1967, has been to encourage municipal development and the independence of local authorities, but to prevent any move towards Palestinian nationalism. The Government did not permit the Mayor of Hebron, Sheikh Ali al-Ja'abari, a courageous patriot, a moderate and cooperative Arab leader, to call a conference of Arab representatives from Bethlehem, Jericho and elsewhere in the occupied territories, so as to establish some sort of Palestinian representation for the Arabs in these territories, other than the P.L.O.'

After this article was written, municipal elections were held in 25 West Bank towns. In all but one case, pro-P.L.O. extremists were elected and the moderates ousted. Among those who lost power was Sheikh Ali al-Ja'abari. This was yet another proof of the folly of Israel holding back at a time when she could have advanced imaginatively — and having to face as a result a far more difficult situation than would have existed if she had chosen the bolder path of recognising the fact that the Palestinians existed as a people, and then dealing with their leaders.

Eliachar and P.M. Levi Eshkol
On June 18, 1967, just after the Six Day War ended, Eliachar wrote to the then Premier, Levi Eshkol, suggesting that Israel should negotiate with the Palestinians, and should even help their leaders to organise the Palestinian entity that undoubtedly existed. Eshkol replied on June 26, 1967, that this was one possible solution to the Middle East problem which was being considered. It was never pursued. 'Then I could have dealt with Arabs whom I knew well,' Eliachar says. 'Now, if those people tried to negotiate with us, they might be shot.

'We have no alternative — we have to negotiate with anybody representing the Palestinians. I think it is a mistake to say "Never!" to Arafat. He has now got world-wide recognition as the representative of the Palestinians. I don't even care if he doesn't officially renounce terror as a weapon prior to talking with us. Once we start talking, the shooting will stop.

'Time is not on our side. The technological gap between us and the Arabs is shrinking. Phantoms, Skyhawks and other modern weapons will not solve our problem. Recent and future development can only make things worse for us — in more ways than one.

'In the international diplomatic and military areas, the dangers lying in wait for us are: growing Sovietization of a number of Arab armies; increased intervention of non-Arab Moslem states; the risk of direct confrontation with the Soviets and the resulting "Vietnamization" of the whole area, with Moscow aiding the guerrilla organisations and the Arab states. The U.S. will be less inclined to come to our aid if we do not abandon fixed attitudes.

'In the social, educational and demographic areas,

too, there are many dangers. A professional Arab class of engineers, doctors, lawyers and scientists is fast increasing in numbers and efficiency. We also have to bear in mind the rapid pace of development in the Arab world today, the huge economic potential of the Arab states, their petroleum dollars and monopoly, and their strides towards unity, notwithstanding abysmal differences between various Arab regimes. All these factors have changed the Arab-Jewish conflict to our detriment.

We Can Only Survive If We Are Accepted by the Arabs
'If we want Israel to survive, we must do all in our power to be accepted by the Arab world. We must seek integration on the chessboard that is the Middle East. Returning "home" to Israel must be synonymous with our return to the Middle East and all that it entails. We must remember that some of the most glorious pages of Jewish history were written in the context of Jewish-Arab cooperation. This does not mean we have to give up Western science and technology. In fact, the Arabs are also "Westernizing" rapidly.

An Exchange of Populations Has Occurred
'Arabs and others, too, must recognize the fact that an exchange of populations has taken place in the Middle East, between Arabs leaving Israel no matter why, and Jews entering Israel from Arab countries. The Arab-Palestinian refugees almost balance to a decimal the Jewish refugees from Arab countries that found a home in Israel. About 650,000 - 700,000 Arabs

left Palestine: about 800,000 Jews from Arab countries entered independent Israel.

'It is deplorable that the Israeli authorities have not stressed this fact more forcefully, comparing it to exchanges of population in India, Pakistan and other lands.

The P.L.O. have stated that their aim is the creation of a "secular democratic state," inhabited by Jews and Arabs practising their various religions. It is curious to note that Arafat's concept is very similar to that of Menahem Begin.

'Begin's vision is of one country, comprising all pre-1967 Israel, plus the occupied territories, in which all inhabitants will have full democratic and religious freedom. He calls this territory Israel, and assumes that it will be dominated by Jews; Arafat offering the same freedoms, calls the same territory Palestine, and assumes Arabs will be in the ascendant. Thus both ideas are essentially the same, and neither will work.

'I reject the whole concept of one state between the Mediterranean and the Jordan River completely. We have seen time and again — in Cyprus, India, Pakistan, Bangladesh, Ireland, all over the world — that trying to make one nation of two races never works. Such a solution is only a guarantee of new trouble.

'*Israel's* raison d'etre *is its Jewishness.* We have wanted our own home for 2,000 years. Our culture and attitude to life, as well as our religion, depend on our having our own state, with an absolute Jewish majority. For that matter, the Palestinians have the same aspirations. Both states should find their places on the checkerboard of the Middle East.

'The whole world has been telling us for years that

the only solution for the Palestinians, for the Middle East, and for us is to create a Palestinian state. But our leaders go on and on blundering about, trying this palliative or that, because they won't face the reality. I believe in the depths of my heart that the core of the problem is to recognise the rights to statehood of both Jews and Palestinians.

Possibility of Harmony

'I believe that Israel, the Palestinians, and eventually Jordan can live together in a harmonious Federation.

'The alternative is self-destruction and annihilation, since both parties to the conflict have or will have the means for it. My credo is: "Let the Israelis live together with the Palestinians and let the Palestinians live together with the Israelis," instead of — "dying like Samson with the Philistines".'

Eliachar also rejects out of hand Dayan's concept of Israel holding the West Bank, while the Arabs there become citizens of Jordan, rather like the South African plan for blacks living in the Transvaal to be citizens of the so-called 'black homelands.'

Other proposals were made by Yigal Allon, the former Foreign Minister, which would have given the West Bankers certain rights, but would have retained the Jordan River as Israel's military boundary. Eliachar describes these as an effort to instal in the Middle East the discredited 'Apartheid' system, tried out in South Africa and Rhodesia, rejected by the blacks in those countries and now condemned by the entire world.

'Nobody will tolerate the creation of such a situation,' he claims, 'And our own Jewish ethics are opposed to it.'

These articles quoted were written by Eliachar before the horrifying civil war between Moslems and Christians broke out in the Lebanon, a land which had previously been cited as an example of how different communities could live happily together. More than ever Eliachar became convinced that it was absurd to suggest that a bi-national Jewish and Arab state could ever exist. The only solution he saw to the Middle East problem was the creation of a separate Palestinian State on the West Bank and in the Gaza Strip.

CHAPTER FOUR

ARMING ARABS

Many people assume, because of the policies that Eliachar is advocating nowadays, that he is an out and out pacifist.

Quite the contrary is true. Eliachar appreciates the importance of the Jews being strong and able to defend themselves as much as does the most fanatical Israeli 'hawk.' During the period of the British Mandate, the Arab riots, and the Jewish state-on-the-way, although he was an official in the Mandatory Government, he was secretly active in the Haganah, the Jewish underground self-defence organisation. He even became one of the 13 members of the Haganah's Supreme Security Council, headed by David Ben-Gurion.

Since the beginning of the twentieth century, the Jews in Palestine had realised they had to fight for their right to exist as a people. They had established a movement known as Hashomer ('The Watchman'). The Haganah was the successor to Hashomer. During the period of the British Mandate, it was an illegal, underground organisation, hunted ruthlessly at times by the British authorities.

The 11 members of the Supreme Security Council were responsible till Statehood for the planning and organisation of the Haganah's activities. Their decisions were vital for Jewish survival. And yet, Jews being Jews, it is hardly surprising that, within the Council, there should be fierce arguments about policies. The majority group, Haganah A, insisted on what was called 'Havlagah' (Self-restraint), which meant adopting a policy of non-retaliation against the Arab population, despite attacks on the Jews by terrorists. The minority group, known as Irgun B, argued that the Jews should retaliate.

In the light of Eliachar's dovelike posture after the State was established one might have expected him to believe in Havlagah. But not a bit of it; he became a member of the higher committee of Irgun B, and opposed the policy of restraint with his usual vigour. Some people may think that this proves that he was always a maverick, 'agin the government,' prone to adopt the unpopular, minority viewpoint.

'Nothing of the kind,' he insists. 'My policy then was completely consistent with my thinking now. I don't say that we should be weak now; on the contrary, we should talk to the Arabs from strength, but we should talk rationally.

'As a native of the country, I understood the Arabs, and I knew that they would interpret Havlagah as weakness. This belief would lead the terrorists among them to intensify their attacks. It was vital to convince the Arabs that the Jews would fight back. I discussed the subject frankly with my Arab friends: I argued that it was in their interest as well as ours to establish that Jewish bloodshed would result in Arab bloodshed, and that force would never deter the Jews. Only reason could solve the differences between the Jews and the Arabs. They agreed with me. I also believed that it was essential to support the opposition among the Arabs to the Grand Mufti Amin El-Husseini and his Supreme Arab Council.

'I tried to explain my point of view to men like Eliyahu Golomb, Dov Hos and Moshe Sharett, but failed, although I did manage to bring Pinhas Rutenberg, the genius who created the Palestine Electric Corporation, to my way of thinking.

'My close friend, Fakhri Nashashibi, one of the leaders of the "Muaridin" (the Arab group opposed to the Mufti's Supreme Arab Council) repeatedly contended that the Haganah and the Jewish national institutions did not understand the Arab mentality. Fakhri told me: "The Mufti's men are striking terrible blows against those Arabs who oppose him. There have been many casualties among the leading Arab families, such as the Nashashibis, the Tukans, the Mayor of Nablus, the Dajanis in Jerusalem, the Shantis in Jaffa. Among those who fell was the son of Sheikh Abd-el-Fatah Darwish. Mustapha, a captain in the Mandatory police, was murdered in Jaffa. Many other Arabs have been killed."

Moderate Arabs Should Defend Themselves
'Fakhri contended that the moderate Arabs were also making a mistake by not reacting with force to the attacks by the agents of the Mufti. He believed that the only practical policy in such a situation was that of an eye for an eye, a tooth for a tooth. But, he pointed out, the Mufti and the Supreme Arab Council had access to the Wakf Moslem sacred funds, and the campaign funds of Moslem communities for holy places in the country, as well as some which the Mufti's men extorted by terrorist means from traders

and men of means. The terrorists' policy was to blackmail the moderate Arabs and attack the Jews. So they had vast sums to finance their activities.

'The Nashashibi party, "Adifa," on the other hand, lacked sources of income. The young men needed money to acquire weapons for self-defence against the Arab terrorists. I told P.R., as we called Rutenberg, that Fakhri had taken me to meet with these young people. Since 1935, we had been holding long discussions with Hassan Sidki Dajani, a lawyer, Fakhri's friend, and an associate of mine since our student days in the French University in Beirut. Hassan Sidki agreed with Fakhri. As long as the Arabs themselves did not take up arms against the Mufti's agents, there would be no peace in the land. They stressed most emphatically in their talks with me that the Mufti's aim was not only to overcome the Jews; he also wanted to become an absolute ruler over the whole of the Arab community, so that he and his henchmen would be recognised as the sole representatives of the Arabs in Palestine.

'Sheikh Abd-el-Fatah Darwish was one of my very close personal friends. We had had many business deals involving land. Through his help I had redeemed large tracts in Jerusalem, part of which today provide the sites for the Knesset, the Government offices, the University, and the Israel Museum. He was one of the most active supporters of the "Adifa" party, headed by Ragheb Bey Nashashibi. The young men in this party were convinced that the Jewish policy of restraint was helping the Mufti to strengthen his hold on the Arabs, and was undermining his opponents. So they asked the Jews for arms to fight the Mufti's men.

'I discussed this request with my colleague in the

Presidium of the Jerusalem Community Council for the Jews, Mr. Haim Salomon. At first he hesitated. He was afraid that placing arms in the hands of young Arabs would serve as a two-edged sword. Again and again I went back and discussed the matter with Fakhri. In the end he convinced me that it was worth taking the risk, so as to strengthen the moderates among the Arabs, those men who had shown tolerance toward the Jews.

'By then I was in a state of near despair: it seemed almost impossible to counter the Mufti's reign of terror. So I decided to discuss the position again with Rutenberg. Since the riots were getting steadily worse, I maintained that it was worth while for the Jews to take risks, and that we should accept Fakhri Nashashibi's proposal. P.R.'s reaction was negative. But I brought up the proposal again and again. We explored it in every possible way, trying to foresee the consequences.

'Finally Rutenberg agreed to recommend it to Eliyahu Golomb and the other leaders of the Haganah. Rutenberg arranged a meeting between Golomb and me. Yaakov Patt, who was in command of the Haganah in the Jerusalem area, also participated in the discussion.

'In spite of differences in outlook regarding parties and classes, my friendship with Yaakov Patt was a very sincere one. Even our conflict in the Haganah Organisation did not cloud our relationship, and we really respected each other.

'The Haganah leaders were convinced by Rutenberg and me, but were not prepared to accept the final responsibility for so hazardous an operation as Jews giving some of their precious arms to Arabs. So they took the proposal to Ben-Gurion himself. Eventually, the Jewish leaders agreed that we should take the chance and put the idea into execution.

'Roads were being attacked by the terrorists from ambushes. I told Fakhri that a consignment of weapons — revolvers, and mortars — would be brought half way to his house in Sheikh Jarrah, at midnight one night, on condition that he and his friends would be responsible for the safe passage home of the Jews bringing the arms. The rendezvous point which Patt fixed was the backyard of the Police Training School, a rather amusing choice.

'Eliahu Sasson, who was then director of the Arab Department of the Jewish Agency, stayed that night at Fakhri's home, in order to be on the spot, and to make sure that the consignment did indeed arrive at its destination, in good order and condition.

'It was a dark, rainy evening. Yaakov Patt and I supervised our men, who carried the weapons in closed boxes, making their way in Indian file along a narrow path through the fields, near a lonely house at the edge of the Bokharan quarter, up to a nearby house where Fakhri's men awaited them. When our boys returned safely, I went up to Sheikh Jarrah to drink a toast with Fakhri and his friends, and with Eliahu Sasson. Fakhri said that within 24 hours we would have proof that the faith placed in him and his men was warranted. We went home towards morning, escorted by Arab guards to the border. Our hearts were heavy with the responsibility we had taken upon ourselves.

'I felt particularly responsible: I had placed my trust in a youngster who was generally regarded as rather frivolous. He loved gaiety, a good time, wine, women and song. Even so, I relied on him. I knew that under the frivolity was a man, who was balanced in his judgment, completely honest, possessed of tremendous courage, loyal and consistent, a man whose word was his bond.

Good News For Arab Moderates — And Jews
'In the early hours of the morning, I reported to Pinhas Rutenberg. We waited for results. Suddenly news spread through Jerusalem that three of the Mufti's men had fallen in a fight with other Arabs. This was the first instance of armed self-defence by the Nashashibis against those who had defiled their family honour, and that of all the other moderate peace-loving Arab families.

'One cannot exaggerate the practical value of this act. But it is only further evidence of the fact that if one wants to live, and maintain peaceful relations, one has to be prepared always to oppose force by force. When the moderates defended themselves with weapons against the heads of the Arab terror, the Arab community and the British were stunned. Until then the opponents of the Supreme Arab Council had suffered injury but were helpless to react in their own defence. The actions of the young men of the "Muaridin" (dissenters) started a chain of counter-attacks.

'A feeling of relief swept over the leaders of Haganah, and the entire community. We felt that we were no longer alone. It cannot be said that the riots or attacks against Jews stopped, but we knew that there had been a turning-point; the very fact that Arab rebels against the Mufti terror had appeared

Fakhri Nashashibi, young moderate Arab leader, killed by the Grand Mufti's assassins in Baghdad. He wrote a 'De Profundis' about the reign of terror imposed on the Arab population by Arab extremists

Rabbi Yehuda Alkalay, first advocate of a Jewish state in Palestine, insisted, 'We must make our country a land of freedom, and proclaim liberty for all its inhabitants, without distinction of religion or nation...'

was a major factor, which the British and the Arabs had to take into account. The stock of the Nashashibi "Adifa" party rose, although its leader, Ragheb (former Mayor of Jerusalem) was at the time a fugitive in Cairo, hiding from the Mufti's murderous henchmen. Together with Hayim Salomon, we went to visit him in his hotel in Heliopolis.

'Many attempts were made to murder Fakhri Nashashibi. He was wounded by a bullet at the entrance to the King David Hotel, and recovered. In the end, an assassin's bullet killed him when he was visiting Baghdad, to gain the support of Nuri Pasha-el-Said, and the Royal House of the Hashemites. On the evening of his departure for Baghdad, he had come to my house in Rehavia to say goodbye. I urged him to postpone his journey until matters were clearer. But in vain. His temerity got the better of him.'

A tragic cry from the heart, which Eliachar calls an Arab *'De Profundis,'* was published at the time by Fakhri Nashashibi in an Arab paper.

A Voice from the Graves of Arab Palestine
'Without exaggeration, one may say that the opponents of the Grand Mufti, Haj Amin el-Husseini, constitute a considerable group in Palestine. They constitute more than half the Arab population of Palestine. But more than 150,000 Arabs have been forced to flee the country from fear of the carnage and the terror organised by the Mufti.

'Not only this. The money collected from the Arab world was not handed over to those whom it was intended to help, but went straight into the pockets of the Mufti's men. Property belonging to the Mufti's opponents, estimated at £4,000,000 was destroyed.

'The roads to the villages and the streets of the towns are paved with the victims of the Husseini terror. Had not kind and merciful people in the country rushed to their aid, those injured by the terror would have been entirely and completely lost. All these horrifying acts, the destruction of life and property, were carried out under deceitful slogans that those affected had sold their lands to the Jews...

'You know Advocate Hassan Sidki Bey el-Dajani well. Would anyone come to testify against him that he had sold even a foot of land to the Jews? Where? When? Dajani saved twenty Arabs from the death sentence imposed by the British Military Court, through his efforts and ability. His reward was that he himself was kidnapped and killed by the murderous gangs of the Mufti.

'This is true too of the house of Rashid in the Nablus district, Faris Alhamallah of Tulkarem, Abd-El-Salam Al-Bekawi, and many others. Did they ever sell land to the Jews? Emissaries of the Mufti have committed abominable acts. Haj Amin el-Husseini uses his dummy, one Aref Abd-El-Razak, who styles himself "Chief leader of the Arab Rebellion in South Syria." This creature sold more than half of the land of Tulkarem to Jews, as well as arms. Let anyone come and deny these facts, if they can...

'From the time of the British occupation until now, we are witness to the fact that his Excellency, Haj Amin el-Husseini, has gained personal benefit from the river of blood gushing from innocent people, who have committed no wrong, but who were abandoned like sheep to the slaughter. They were sacrificed to enrich the Mufti's henchmen. Does "his honour" remember the price he had to pay for acquiring the office of Mufti in Palestine, and how much his post of Head of the Supreme Moslem Council cost the country? I do not think that he has managed to forget the number of his victims sacrificed in order to strengthen his chair of office and to establish the basis for his claim to his position in the Moslem Council.

'This office has cost Palestine more than 3,000 Arab lives, human beings who have departed this world, and are now complaining before Allah about the hypocrisy of their oppressors!'

CHAPTER FIVE

ONE LAND, TWO NATIONS

Most histories of Zionism and modern Palestine tend to start with the arrival on the scene of the first wave of Eastern European immigrants, the Biluim, who came in 1880, and to move from there to the arrival of Theodor Herzl, the prophet of Zionism. On this interpretation, there were no Jews who mattered living in Palestine before the Central and Eastern European Jews came. And there never was such a creature as a Palestine Arab.

Eliachar sees things rather differently, perhaps because of his vantage point, that of a sixteenth generation 'sabra.' On the one hand he maintains that Jews were never interlopers from Europe who pushed their way into Palestine; on the contrary, many Jews had been there all the time. On the other hand, he recognises the validity of the Palestinian Arabs' claim to a national identity.

According to his interpretation of history, the Arab Liberation Movement was initiated in Egypt in the nineteenth centry. It spread to Syria, Iraq, Lebanon and Palestine, countries which were formerly part of the Ottoman Empire. The struggle of the Balkan peoples to throw off the Turkish yoke, and the revolt of the Mahdi in the Sudan, contributed to the Arab awakening. Active underground organisations were formed. The Arab nationalists opposed both the Turkish regime and the Christian conquerors, the unbelievers who had reached their lands. The Young Turks Movement also had a great influence on the emergence of Arab nationalism.

'The Zionist Revival,' Eliachar says, 'developed as a combination of centuries old Jewish visions and the aspirations to liberty of small European nations, which characterized the nineteenth century.'

The Zionist Predecessor of Herzl, Rabbi Yehuda Alkalay

Jews whose families had lived for generations in Palestine realised long before the European Jews that the Palestinian Arabs had national aspirations, according to Eliachar. Most of these Jews were Sephardis, who understood the Arabs. One of the most notable of the early dreamers of a revival of the Jewish homeland was Rabbi Yehuda Alkalay, a Sephardi rabbi born in Sarajevo, who came to Jerusalem with his parents when he was six years old. He died in Jerusalem in 1878.

A great scholar and a prolific writer, he was the first advocate of the creation of a Jewish state in Palestine as a solution to the problem of anti-Semitism in Eastern Europe. Not only did he set out a detailed programme in his writings for the revival of the state, he also travelled all over Europe trying to get support for his idea of getting a charter from the Ottoman sultan to establish a Jewish state. Theodor Herzl's grandfather was a member of his community in Zemlyn, Serbia, at one stage, and he may have mentioned his ideas to young Theodor. Certainly, Herzl's 'Jewish State,' written 60 years after Rabbi Alkalay proposed his plan for the Jewish renascence, duplicated many of his ideas.

Unlike Herzl, however, Rabbi Alkalay considered the position of the Palestinian Arabs. He insisted: 'We must make our country a land of freedom, and proclaim liberty for all its inhabitants, without distinction of religion or nation...'

Early Warnings to Zionists

Eliachar goes on, 'Another Jerusalemite who foresaw the need to develop proper relations with the Arabs was the great educator, Nissim Bekhar, who founded the first modern school in Jerusalem, the Alliance Israelite Universelle. He wrote, "The two nations, the Arab and the Jewish, are brothers, and it is up to us to try to win their hearts. After each Arab understands us he will give us his hand and will say, 'You are my brother.' We have neglected this matter, and I grieve because of this neglect."

'Jerusalem-born Professor Abraham Shalom Yehudah, the only Jerusalem Jew at Herzl's first Zionist Congress in 1897, also pleaded for cooperation between Jews and Arabs from the very beginning. Already at that Congress he warned Herzl about the existence of the Arabs in Eretz Israel.'

Many other Sephardi Jews tried to strengthen Jewish-Arab ties in the early days, but the influence of the European Jews was too strong.

After the British occupation in 1917, Eliachar recalls, an intellectual group known as 'Pioneers of the East,' of which he was later the president, was formed by young Sephardi Jews. They invited Arabs to join them in discussions. They also encouraged the teaching of

Arabic among Jews, and of Hebrew among Arabs. Their club was the first youth club established in Jerusalem. Through this cooperative effort some young Arabs learned Hebrew, and some of them remained good friends of the Jews. One of these was Advocate Rashid Hadad.

Another Arab who sought mutual understanding through 'The Pioneers of the East' was Akram Tokan, who published a pamphlet, 'Hidden Truths.' In it the writer reminisces about former Jewish-Arab cooperative activity, suggests likely avenues towards understanding and peace, and towards building and strengthening Jewish-Arab brotherhood. In the 'thirties, Aref El-Assali published a pamphlet called 'Arabs and Jews in History.' He begins his preface with the words: 'This pamphlet was written because in our opinion it is vital to highlight the connections between the two nations, Jews and Arabs alike. The links are racial, historic, and social, in spite of the artificial strangeness and separation between them, which are essentially the result of political causes...'

With the rise in Arab opposition, some Jews in Palestine, Sephardis and Ashkenazis, founded the association 'Kadimah' ('Forwards'), at Mikveh Yisrael in 1936, under Chief Rabbi Ben-Zion Uziel and David Yellin.

Christian Hatred
In the light of what was to happen in Lebanon in 1975 and 1976, it is ironical, Eliachar notes, that much of the opposition to the Jews in Palestine was stirred up by Christian Arabs, most of them educated in Beirut.

Immediately after the conquest of Palestine by General Edmund Allenby in World War I, the British administrators of the Mandate over the country, who did not see eye to eye with the policy of their government in London, as laid down in the Balfour Declaration, set out to turn Jew against Arab and Arab against Jew, so as to maintain British power through classic 'Divide and Rule' tactics. Eliachar saw these schemes at first hand, as he was serving at the time in the administration.

He had already discovered, while an officer in the Turkish army, that pro-Arab Americans and Arab Christian elements in the American University in Beirut and in the French Jesuit University in the Lebanon were preaching anti-Semitism. They aimed thereby to increase the influence of Christianity in the Middle East and to foster the national interests of their countries.

Christian-Arab graduates from the universities believed that they enjoyed the support of many of the British officers. Journals like 'El Carmel' and 'Falastine,' produced by the Christians, tried to rouse national fanaticism and Arab hatred of the Jews.

Eliachar says, 'Two Christian brothers named Bustrous were particularly venomous. They were pharmacists, who had studied at the American University in Beirut. They owned a pharmacy in Jaffa, in the street bearing their family name. These two were notorious for their hatred of the Jews. They had a hand in every movement, even the smallest, working against Jewish settlement in the country. Every Zionist problem that arose was dealt with by them in books and newspapers. Thus they became known as "experts" on Zionism.

'They got to know many Jews serving with them in the Turkish army. Paradoxically, it was they who showed me how much pro-Zionist literature abounded in English; more than once they argued that the British Christians were more enthusiastic about the Zionist ideal than the Jews themselves, both because of their affinities with the Bible and their view of Imperial interests.

'Many years later, as the Arab national movement strengthened, Christian Lebanese leaders began to fear for their status, and came to think that a strong Jewish community on the borders of Lebanon might be helpful to them. But it was already too late. They had sown the wind, and they reaped the whirlwind. The subsequent Lebanese agony of the mid-'seventies was a terrible retribution for the shortsighted, anti-Semitic preachings of the Christian Arabs.'

CHAPTER SIX

MISTAKES OF THE ZIONIST LEADERSHIP

'Looking back over half-a-century of Arab-Jewish relations in the Holy Land,' Eliachar says with regret, 'I must admit that it was not only chauvinistic Arabs or scheming British administrators or the hatred of Christian anti-Semitic teachers that caused the splits between the two peoples. Serious mistakes were also made by the Zionist Organisation, which did not realise the importance of working with the Arabs, and, I sometimes think, never lost an opportunity to antagonize them.'

I put to Eliachar the fact that Dr. Chaim Weizmann went to great pains to cultivate the friendship and support of Emir Feisal, the son of Sherif Hussein of Mecca, and the leader of the Arab revolt sponsored by T. E. Lawrence during World War I. Feisal was considered by the world to be the spokesman for the Arabs at the Peace Conference after the War. Weizmann's negotiations with Feisal culminated in Feisal sending a letter to Felix Frankfurter, a member of the American Zionist deputation, on March 3, 1919 in which Feisal wrote, among other things: 'We feel that the Arabs and the Jews are cousins in race, suffering similar oppressions at the hands of powers stronger than themselves, and by a happy coincidence have been able to take the first steps towards the attainment of their national ideals together. We Arabs, especially the educated among us, look with the deepest sympathy on the Zionist Movement... We will do our best, insofar as we are concerned, to help them through; we will wish the Jews a most hearty welcome home...'

It is true that later the Sherif and almost all his descendants were dethroned. King Hussein of Jordan is the only Hashemite still in power. Despite the unfortunate fate of the Hashemites, I asked Eliachar, what more could Weizmann have done than obtain the support of Feisal, the acknowledged leader of the Arab delegation at the Peace Conference?

'I must concede that Dr. Chaim Weizmann did try at first to make contact with eminent Arab leaders,' answered Eliachar. 'He did have the important meetings with Emir Feisal and the Emir Abdullah, two Arab leaders of very great importance, to which you refer. But all too soon he found that his hands were being tied by the British. This is the reason for the inconsistencies one detects in his writings and thoughts in all matters affecting the Arab question. At times he tried to draw near to the Arabs, then he retreated. To this vacillating policy his advisers in the movement contributed.'

Not everybody was blind to the danger of ignoring the reality of the Arab presence and Arab aims. Eliachar outlines some of the efforts made by Jews to counter the official blindness.

'There was a time when young people, born in the country, such as Ittamar Ben-Avi (the son of Eliezer Ben-Yehudah, the propagator of Hebrew), Asher Sapir, Ovadiah Camhi, and Jacques Calmi, who was Weizmann's private secretary, worked hard to help Weizmann to form ties with eminent Palestinian and other

Arab leaders. Prominent members of the Sephardi community came forward with suggestions to draw the two nations closer together.

'At the time I was the representative of the Organisation of Young Sephardim, from which evolved the Organisation of Pioneers of the East. From the end of 1921, when I returned from my studies abroad, I joined in the effort to make the Zionist leaders cooperate with the Arabs.

'At the beginning there were some people in the leadership who had had considerable contact with Arabs. These men included Moise de Picciotto; General Bianchini, a Jewish scholar and Orientalist, of Italian origin; Rabbi de Sola Poole, a famous American who had settled in Jerusalem for a period as a member of the first Zionist mission to Palestine after the British conquest in World War I.

'But all our efforts came to no avail because of the consistent opposition of other Zionist leaders around Weizmann.

'The Sephardi Rabbis — the acknowledged leaders of the Jews in Palestine until 1917 — realised the danger inherent in this lack of understanding, and the absence of a policy of rapprochement with our neighbours. In their public appearances, and in their meetings with the heads of the Zionist Organisation, they expressed their anxiety. The Chief Rabbi, First in Zion, Jacob Meir, in his speech at the 13th Zionist Congress at Carlsbad, 1923, told the delegates: "It cannot be denied that the Sephardi Jews, being native to the country, and knowing the language and customs of the Arabs, could help a great deal in this matter. Many Sephardi and Arab leaders came to me with a request that we should try to bring about peace, should organise joint projects with Arabs. It is still not too late. The position can be remedied through new exertions by the Zionist leadership, with the purpose of bringing all those who have the power and ability to help us in building our national home."

Possible Links With Arab Movements

'Dr. Yitzchak Levi, a banker, Dr. Nissim Malul, and Rabbi Y. M. Toledano, later Minister of Religions in Israel, all demanded that Arabic newspapers should be produced by the Jews to work for better understanding. Had our leaders of the Movement been wise enough to respond to this advice they could have tried at least to build bridges to the Arabs without harming our national movement.

'In fact, to my knowledge, the heads of the Arab movements in neighbouring countries were eager to come to an agreement with the Zionist Movement. I was in touch with all the different streams in the Arab movements, and I received reliable information, even secret information, about all that was going on in these circles.

'I had frequent meetings with the leaders of the Jewish communities in the Arab countries. They were dedicated Zionists, who believed with all their hearts that there was a bright future for Jews and Arabs in the area, if the two peoples would only get together to consider common problems with understanding. The leading Sephardis were in constant touch with the heads of the Arab movements.

'From the very beginning of my service with the Mandatory Government in Palestine, I established firm contacts with Arab intellectuals, both Moslem and

Christian. Among my close friends were the El-Ansari, Mishel Makhluf,, Khuri, Cavalcanti, Ha'ashem, and Tokan families. And I worked closely with my colleague Ajaje Naweihad, a Druse, clever and educated, and a proud nationalist. He was a gifted writer, who translated many books from English to Arabic, especially the works of Rosita Forbes, the famous explorer of the Sahara Desert.

'At the beginning of the 'twenties, Ajaje disclosed to me his fears that a bloody struggle might develop between Jews and Arabs, not through any fault of the Arabs but because of the attitudes of the Zionist leaders from Europe. As a learned man, Ajaje was well read in both Jewish and Arabic literature, and it was amazing to him that the descendants of the great Hebrew scholars, philosophers, poets and theologians of the Spanish, Egyptian, and North African eras, all of whom wrote in Arabic (in Hebrew lettering), found no echo among those who wanted to renew national life in a region, which was chiefly Arab.

'After I left my post in the Mandatory Government, I became the representative of many large Egyptian companies which were active in finance, export, import, and manufacture. One of these companies was a very well-known firm, Société d'Avances Commerciales. Among its directors were eminent men like J. H. Peretz, one of the founders of the Stock Exchange in Cairo, Alfred Cohen of Tunis, and Ovadiah Salem of Salonika. All of them had been educated in the schools of the Alliance Israelite Universelle. Many had even taught there, and later set up associations and companies jointly; these constituted a sort of Egyptian industrial and financial empire. Through them, I came into direct contact too with outstanding leaders in the economy, heads of the Egyptian national company "Misr," which slowly, surely and firmly began to penetrate into agriculture, commerce, industry, banking, shipping, and civil aviation.

'More than once, these Jewish leaders came to Jerusalem, and pleaded with the Zionist leaders to adopt a more reasonable approach to the Arabs.

'Among those who strove for better understanding between Jews and Arabs was advocate Leon Castro, Editor of the newspaper "La Liberté" of the WAFD, Zaghlul Pasha's Liberation Party. Castro had been involved in the WAFD from his youth. For a period he had also been the leader of the Zionist movement in Egypt. He saw the absolute necessity to establish closer relations between Zionists and Arab nationalists, and even believed that the leaders of Egypt could be of great help in promoting better understanding between us and our Arab neighbours in Palestine. Others like him were the editors of the paper "Israel," Dr. Albert Mosseri and his wife Mazal, daughter of the Palestine Supreme Court judge, Malkiel Many. The paper "L'Aurore" as well, edited by Y. Sciotto, made endeavours to promote better ties between Jews and Arabs. Influential Jews also worked on other papers, like "Al Ahram," "Al Mukattam," the "Egyptian Gazette," and the "Bourse Egyptienne."

'Unfortunately, the warning of these fervent Zionists, and many others like them, were ignored by the official leadership.

'In my dealings with some of the Eastern European leaders of the Yishuv (Jewish Community) and the Zionist Movement, I heard many excuses for the short-sighted policy with regard to the Arabs. One argument was that these leaders feared that the

Jewish minorities would be assimilated by the Arabs, and the ideals of the renascence and re-settlement of the National Home would be dimmed, if Zionism allied itself to the Arab liberation movements. There were other arguments, less serious, echoes of which are still heard today. Some were worried about the alleged danger of the "Levantinization" of the Jews in Palestine, if they tried to integrate with the Arabs of the country and the region.'

Ussishkin: "There's No Arab Problem"
'When Menahem Ussishkin, one of the very top Zionist leaders, came to Jerusalem, at the end of World War I, as Chairman of the Zionist Commission, my colleagues and I, of the Pioneers of the East, visited him. We raised the "Arab Problem." Ussishkin beetled his brows and answered: "For me, and for us, the Jewish people, there exists only and solely the Jewish Problem. There is no such thing as an Arab Problem."

'Tactless remarks were made in public by our leaders. These were turned into slogans in hostile Arab mouths, and were used to incite the crowds against us. One well-known example is Dr. Weizmann's famous claim that "the purpose of the Zionist Movement is to establish a State in Eretz Israel, as Jewish as England is English!" This pronouncement in itself expressed an honest aspiration. But it caused confusion. Among the intellectual Arabs of Palestine and the neighbouring countries, Weizmann's words were harped on and reiterated. It was considered to be proof that the Arabs could not place any reliance on the Zionist Movement's pious declarations of a desire for co-existence between the two nations.

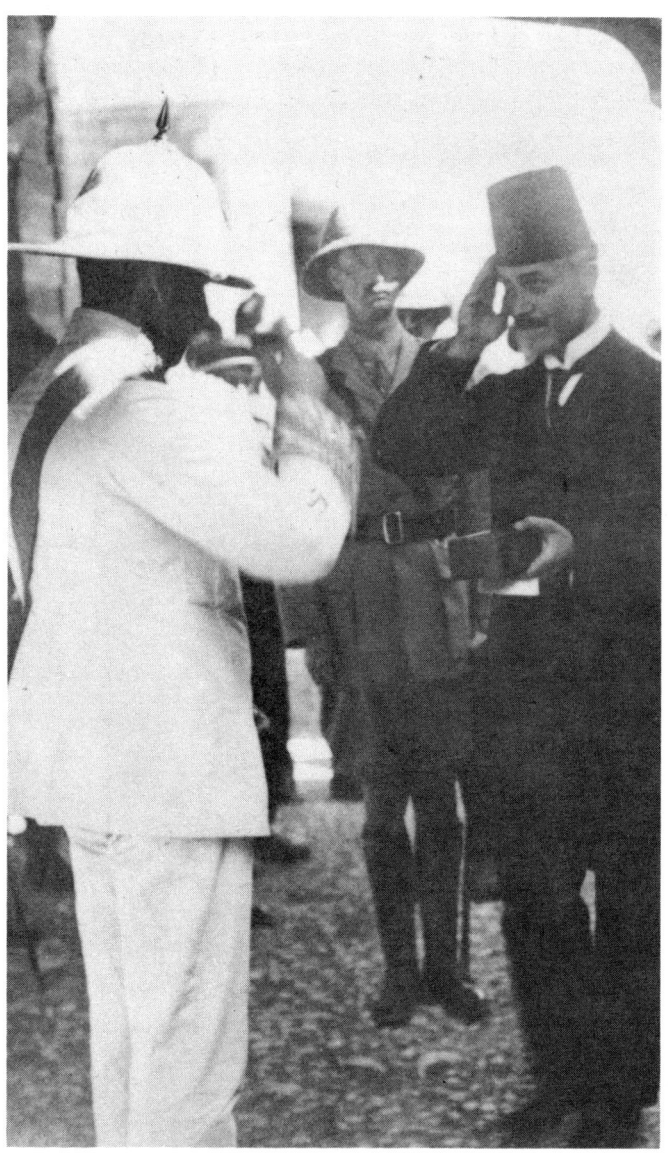

Ragheb Bey Nashashibi, Mayor of Jerusalem, salutes Lord Samuel. Later he warned Moshe Sharett that the Jews had 'introduced a snake into the inside pocket of your coat,' when they supported Dr. Hussein Khaldi for the mayoralty of Jerusalem.

Dr. Judah L. Magnes, Chancellor of the Hebrew University of Jerusalem, founder of the Ihud, believed in a bi-national state in which Jews would be a permanent minority. Elie Eliachar disagreed

'The Jewish revival in its own homeland required the rebirth of the Hebrew language and the renascence of Hebrew culture. I for one never questioned that these needs existed. But, from the necessity to develop our own culture, most of our leaders inferred that we had to separate completely from the Arabs. In spite of the lack of means, our leaders pressed on with their separatist policy in education. Many Arab teachers and educators spoke to me openly and emphatically about the fact that the whole purpose of Jewish education was to set up an entity cut off from the rest of the inhabitants of the country and region. Moreover, the struggle of our labour movement to establish Jews as labourers, and not as employers using Arab labour, involved denying Arabs the right to work on Jewish projects. This deepened the feeling of estrangement among the Arabs in "their own country" — and justified, so our opponents argued, their concern for their future.

'Far be it from me to detract from the achievements of our leaders. Hebrew education and Jewish labour were vital for the rebirth of the nation, they made possible our progress towards independence. But, if we want to be honest with ourselves, and to look at the Arab problem objectively, we must admit that any other people would have reacted to such developments just as the Arabs did.'

Eliachar then moves on to review another Arab grievance, which was completely ignored by the Jewish leaders, because they considered the complaint to be groundless and irrational.

'Considerable bitterness was caused among the most simple of the Arab masses, the tenant farmers, who complained about the acquisition of land by the

Zionist Movement. The Jews paid the Arab landowners enormous prices for every square foot of ground that was acquired. On the other hand, insufficient thought was given to the future of the tenant-farmers, who soon squandered the little money they received as compensation from the landowners. They were evicted, and deprived of their normal livelihood. The argument that the legal owners of the land had been paid out so high a price did not console them.

'We Jews did little to dispel their accumulating bitterness. There were people in the country, chiefly the Sephardi Jews, who were the main proponents of reasonable solutions. From the time of the very first Jewish settlement outside the walls of Jerusalem, the Sephardis had had experience in acquiring lands from Arabs. Many deals had been concluded by veteran, well-known Sephardi families like the Amzalaks, the Navons, the Moyals, the Manys, the Chelouches and the Eliachars. We were all known and trusted by the Arabs, rich and poor alike. We also acted as trustees for the Jewish national organisations, which, as non-Ottomans, were not allowed to buy land.

'The PICA (Palestine Jewish Colonial Association) of the Rothschilds, and the ICA (Jewish Colonial Association) of Baron de Hirsch had learned that it was worth while to make use of Sephardi Jews in carrying out land negotiations with Arabs. Herzl himself wrote in his novel "Old New Land" that he sent "Alladino" to Eretz Israel to acquire lands. His fictional "Alladino" is a Sephardi who speaks Arabic and Greek, a reliable, sharp-witted man, a member of one of the proud families whose ancestry can be traced back to the days of the Expulsion from Spain.

We knew that the tenants as well as the owners had to be considered.

'All that I have said does not imply, of course, that the Jews should not have acquired land in Israel. Nor does it reduce by one iota our right to return to the homeland of our forefathers, all the more since so much of the land was uninhabited and deserted when the Zionist revival began. Large areas consisted of marshes and stony wastes. But we should have given thought to those uprooted from the soil, tenant-farmers, whose families had occupied certain regions for generations.

'The Sephardi leaders could have given considerable guidance on this sensitive point, but, unfortunately, our experience was ignored. When I personally acquired land from Arabs, I entered into negotiations, not only with the owners, but also with the tenants. I took great care to make arrangements which satisfied the needs of these tenant farmers as well as the desires of the owners to get good prices. Generally, I acquired good farming land for the tenants in other places.

Unfamiliarity and Contempt
'The heads of the Zionist Movement were not familiar with the mentality of the Arab, his customs, even what he considered to be elementary good manners. Thus many blows were struck, unconsciously, against Arab sensitivities. Even in the very first year after the conquest of Jerusalem by General Allenby in 1917, when the Arab leaders were still responding to invitations from the Jews to participate in functions, more than once the guests left in great

indignation, since there was no one to accord them proper respect and honour. Weizmann held a great reception for General Allenby in the Hafetz mansion in the Bokharan quarter in Jerusalem. There was no one there to greet the Moslem Mayor of Jerusalem, or the Grand Mufti, or the Sheikh of the Mosque of Omar, or the Cadi (the Moslem religious judge). Not only were they ignored on arrival, they were also seated at the back. They left the hall in fury.

'As I have mentioned before, two days after the capture of Jerusalem, my father was appointed Deputy Mayor by the British. He was a witness to a similar incident, when he tried to develop a closer relationship between Mussa Kazem Pasha el-Husseini, the then Mayor, and the heads of our community.

'When Menahem Ussishkin arrived in the country as Chairman of the Zionist Commission, my father tried to get him to meet Mussa Kazem Pasha. The accepted custom, of course, was that visitors should call on the Mayor. Ussishkin wouldn't do this. As a personal favour to my father, the Mayor agreed to go with him to Ussishkin.

'When they arrived, they were left waiting in the corridor outside Ussishkin's office for a long time. Eventually Mussa Kazem Pasha, a proud man, accustomed to the etiquette usual among statesmen, aware of his status and the respect due to him, left in high dudgeon, angry not only with Ussishkin, but also with my father, his friend and partner in business since the time of the Turks, for exposing him to such insults.

'Anyone reading about these incidents today may imagine that they were passing, trivial matters. But it is precisely theses codes of behaviour that create the right atmosphere to make friendly relations between people possible. From this point of view, we have still not learned a lesson.

'Fostering close relations between people, and especially between people of different nations, is not only a criterion of cultural standards, but it also has important political consequences. A man may be well-versed in the history of a people, but, if he cannot create the right atmosphere for rapprochement, all his learning will be of no avail.'

Eliachar points out that every state nowadays takes great care to provide its emissaries with full knowledge about the conventions and manners of other peoples, and that close attention is paid to sentiments and sensitivities. The development of a comprehensive intelligence network is not confined to military matters only, but embraces all aspects of behaviour, as well as political and economic trends.

He says that, in the days of the Ottoman rule, the leaders of the Zionist Movement consulted the Sephardi leaders in Palestine. After the British conquest of Palestine in World War I, this practice was abandoned, as the 'Anglo-Saxon' and Eastern leaders became stronger and stronger. Very likely, their subconscious thinking was that, just as the government had passed from Turkey to Britain, so the leadership in Palestine had passed from the Sephardi Jews living there for years to the Jews of Great Britain, the U.S.A., and the European countries. Their conviction that they knew best was strengthened because they were the people with the money.

'To this day there are many people who remember the cooperation between Sephardis and Ashkenazis, in the old days in Palestine. But, since 1918, the

Sephardis and the Ashkenazis rooted in Palestine and the surrounding Arab countries, have been pushed aside. They are ignored as if they have ceased to exist', Eliachar claims.

'I remember this in connection with an election to the Jerusalem municipality during the Mandatory Period. According to Mandatory rules, the mayor had to be an Arab. The heads of the Sephardi community proposed that the Jews should support Ragheb Bey Nashashibi for the role of mayor. He was opposed by the Arab extremists. We Sephardis argued that the Jews should not contribute to his defeat, because we knew that he was one of the most moderate among the Arabs in his attitude to the Jews.

Socialists Back the Wrong Party
'Moshe Sharett decided, in consultation with the other heads of the Zionist Movement, that Jews, believers in socialism and other liberal causes, should support the so-called progressives among the Arabs — the intellectuals, the pseudo-left-wingers — as against the conservatives. Incredible as it may seem, Jewish leaders encouraged the rise of the notables of the Husseini clan, who were to cause us so much misery. Sharett and others instructed the Jews to support Dr. Hussein Khaldi for the mayoralty of Jerusalem. Khaldi was elected, and Ragheb was defeated.

'I played a very active role opposing this mistaken policy, because I was convinced that we should on no account turn our backs on the moderate element. If we did, we ourselves, with our own hands, would be alienating moderate Arab leaders in Jerusalem, Jaffa, and Nablus, who had ties with the Nashashibi family, and the "Adifa" party. These Arabs constituted the opposition to the Mufti, who was our bitter enemy. I remember a fateful meeting we Sephardi leaders had with Colonel Kisch, Chairman of the Jewish Agency Executive, and Moshe Sharett. We tried desperately to convince them that it was our national duty to stand by the moderates against the extremists, but our arguments fell on deaf ears.

'After the election of Dr. Hussein Khalidi, I happened to be at the King David Hotel, together with Ragheb Bey Nashashibi and Fakhri Nashashibi. As we left, we encountered Moshe Sharett. After shaking hands with Sharett with customary Eastern courtesy and formality — which does not reveal at all what a man is really thinking — Ragheb said to Sharett: "Your success will cost you and the rest of the Jews much, not because the Nashashibis will feel vindictive. We shall control our desire to treat you as you have treated us, because of our friendship with our brothers with whom we grew up" (and he pointed at us, his Sephardi friends). "You Jews will suffer because of the snake you have introduced into the inside pocket of your coat, without realising what you have done to yourselves."

'One cannot say that any serious or imaginative consideration was given by our leaders to establishing a firm and friendly relationship with the Arabs. Following on the Arab riots of 1929, a joint office of Jewish institutions in Palestine was founded, consisting of representatives of the Jewish Agency, the National Council, and Agudat Israel. This office was headed by Colonel Kisch, representing the Agency Executive, Yitzhak Ben-Zvi of the Va'ad Leumi, later Israel's second president; H. M. Kalvarisky; and my father, Yitzhak Shmaya Eliachar. But the body proved to be helpless, and I remember to this day how distressed my late father was about it.

'On February 26, 1930, the office took a number of decisions intended to improve matters. Among other things, it was decided that efforts must be made to weaken the incitement against the Jews and against Zionism in Arab newspapers, both in Palestine and in neighbouring countries, and that we must work towards stopping or diminishing the influence of the Grand Mufti in Jerusalem. He was inciting the Arab masses against the Jews. The Kisch Committee called for strengthening economic activity between the two nations, and also called on the Jews "not to declare a public ban on Arab labour, and not to work in a systematic and organised fashion to push the Arabs out of Jewish enterprises." It also urged the establishment of a newspaper in Arabic, and of loan funds to provide small loans to Arab Fellahin. Nothing came of these proposals.'

Among other suggestions for solving the Arab-Jewish problem made at the time was a 'canton' idea, propounded by Ittamar Ben-Avi, and the concept of the Seventh Dominion supported by Zeev Jabotinsky and his followers.

There was also a suggestion of a population exchange as a solution, especially to the tenant farmer problem. St. John Philby of Arabia proposed this idea to Weizmann, Ben-Gurion and others. The most active of the supporters of this scheme was Edward Norman, founder of the Norman Fund for Culture in the 'thirties. He and Eliachar operated from the office of the Palestine Electric Corporation in London, along with Pinhas Rutenberg, and even sent Jewish and non-Jewish emissaries abroad to try to put this idea of population exchange into practice, especially in Syria and Iraq.

However, nothing tangible was achieved. Every so often these ideas were reborn, blossomed, died. Many memoranda were lodged with leaders of the Zionist Movement, and with everyone responsible for administering matters in Palestine and in the Movement. Various people wrote on the subject of Arab-Jewish relations at length.

Eliachar respected the proponents of these ideas but noted a weakness in their approach. The moderates, like the extremists, suffered from their reliance on abstract theories, acquired through reading books or through superficial contacts, without any real experience of day-to-day life with Arab neighbours. They lacked the ground under their feet acquired through living together for generations; men in organisations like the 'Ihud' and 'Brit Shalom', formed to promote understanding between Jews and Arabs, came to their conclusions by way of theoretical analysis and not through practice. And the extremists ignored the Arab problem altogether, not trying to understand it or to seek any solution at all to it.

Morris D. Hexter, the representative of the Marshal group in 1929, when the Jewish Agency was founded, told Eliachar in 1948 that on his first visits to Egypt and the Arab lands of the Middle East, he had been struck by the important positions held by the Jewish communities there, and their political influence. He had suggested using them as go-betweens between the Zionist Movement and Arabs towards peace and understanding, but was warned off by the Executive of the Jewish Agency on the ground that his idea might have bad effects on the future of the National Home.

Several leaders of the Zionist Movement, and important thinkers, such as Joseph Klausner, opposed the teaching of Arabic in our schools, on the ground that this could lead to Jewish assimilation into the surrounding Arab culture. Dr. Arthur Ruppin, a sociologist, claimed that he had investigated the problem thoroughly, and had reached the conclusion that it was not possible for Jews and Arabs in Palestine to have a common language, or a common life, and that the question in the end would have to be decided by force. Joseph Brenner, the socialist writer, came to a similar conclusion.

'For these reasons,' wrote Eliachar in one article, 'the Zionist Movement, and especially the extremists, came to believe that only by developing Jewish strength would we be able to survive in Palestine and the region. It did not occur to anyone that the day was not far off when the Arabs in the countries around us would be fired with national resistance to the colonial ruler. No informed person even dreamed, at that time, that within a few years, a few decades of bygone yesterdays, England and France would lose their colonial holdings in the whole Middle East. Nobody suspected that these mighty empires would descend from their heights to become second or third grade powers.'

The Ihud
Dramatic hope of reaching some kind of rapprochement with Arabs arose when some of the foremost Jews in Palestine, led by Dr. Judah L. Magnes, the

revered Chancellor of the Hebrew University, created a movement known as the Ihud (Union). Eliachar attended the founding meeting in the home of Abraham Goldwater, a co-director of his in the Palestine Milling and Trading Co. Ltd. Dr. Magnes, who chaired the first meeting, suggested that Eliachar, by virtue of his contacts with the Arabs, should undertake the leadership of the association, but Eliachar insisted that Magnes was so widely respected everywhere in the world that he was the ideal head of the Ihud.

Later Dr. Magnes produced his plan for peace — he wanted to stipulate that the Jews would never become more than 40 per cent of the population of Palestine, thereby appeasing the fears of the Arabs, even the extremists. Eliachar opposed this plan vehemently; he could not accept that the Jews could voluntarily, of their own free will, accept a limitation on the right of Jews to immigrate to their homeland, or to become a majority there. Dr. Magnes would not budge, and eventually Eliachar left the Ihud, although he remained on the best of terms with Dr. Magnes.

CHAPTER SEVEN

ARAB RIOTS AND THE PEEL COMMISSION

Arab riots broke out in Palestine on several occasions during the thirty years of the British control of the country, between 1918 and 1948. In 1920 the riot in Jerusalem very much resembled the pogroms which the Jews had known in Russia, since the British authorities seemed to be on the side of the rioters. Thus, when a group of Jews under Vladimir Jabotinsky defended themselves against the mobs, they were arrested, and Jabotinsky was sentenced to 15 years imprisonment, a sentence which was later quashed. Six Jews were killed.

Much more serious riots took place in 1929, starting as a result of Arab objections to Jews having access to the Western Wall to pray. Nearly 150 Jews were killed, and the venerable community of Hebron was destroyed. The reaction of the British Government was summed up by Beatrice Webb, the famous socialist wife of Sidney Webb, who had become Lord Passfield, the Colonial Secretary, responsible for Palestine. She said, 'I can't understand why the Jews make such a fuss over a few dozen of their people killed in Palestine. As many are killed every week in traffic accidents, and no one pays any attention.'

Passfield sent a commission headed by Sir John Hope Simpson to investigate the situation. He reported that there was 'no room in Palestine to swing a cat,' and that the country did not have the economic absorptive capacity to take in thousands of Jews. Acting on this report, Passfield issued a White Paper, suspending Jewish immigration and curtailing the acquisition of land by Jews.

Weizmann resigned, and the resultant storm of protest overwhelmed the weak British labour government. Not only the Jews, but leading Englishmen like Stanley Baldwin and Leopold Amery, and world figures like General Jan Smuts of South Africa, castigated the Government for its betrayal of the Balfour Declaration by the issue of the Passfield White Paper. The Prime Minister, Ramsay Macdonald, surrendered, and virtually repudiated Passfield in a letter written to Weizmann, which, in effect, nullified the White Paper.

The decade that followed was dominated by the rise of Adolf Hitler. In terms of the Macdonald letter, thousands of German Jews, escaping from Germany, entered Palestine, bringing with them a wave of productivity and prosperity. But in 1936 the Arabs rioted again, this time so seriously that the rioting turned into the Arab Revolt, which lasted for several years.

The riots, instigated by Haj Amin el-Husseini, the Grand Mufti, began with a general strike and the murder of some Jews. But the killing soon assumed massive proportions. The toll of casualties, both Jews and Arabs, soared into the hundreds, then the thousands.

The British Government sent substantial military forces to Palestine to deal with this Arab Revolt. It also appointed a Royal Commission, headed by Lord Peel, to investigate not only the cause of the riots, but the entire situation in Palestine.

Dr. Chaim Weizmann's evidence before the Commission is considered to be a classic exposition of the Zionist cause. He spoke for more than two hours of a people 'who were a minority everywhere, a majority nowhere, to some extent identified with the races among which it lives, but is still not quite identical. It is a disembodied ghost of a race, and it inspires suspicion, and suspicion breeds hatred. There should be one place in the world, in God's wide world, where we could live and express ourselves in accordance with our own character, and make our contribution to civilisation in our own way, and through our own channels.'

In the light of the claims now advanced by Menahem Begin, Golda Meir and others that there was never such a thing as a Palestinian entity, and that the concept was only invented after the Six Day War in June, 1967, it is only fair to note the arguments advanced by the Palestinian Arabs to the Peel Commission in 1936.

They contended that Palestine was an Arab country before the Turks conquered it, that they had not been consulted about the Balfour Declaration and the Mandate, and that the influx of the Jews had endangered their national status.

Eliachar did not address the Commission, because, he says, he did not represent any official body, but he did submit a written memorandum, in English, which he called, 'A Jew in Palestine Before the Royal Commission.' In it he presented a comprehensive view of the country as it was at the time, as seen through the eyes of a Jew born and bred in Palestine. Four decades later, it is still a remarkable document, both because of the accuracy of the analysis and the breadth of his vision for both Jews and Arabs.

In the course of his long presentation, Eliachar wrote,

'There is one fundamental human right and that is to live and develop. No one is begrudging this to the Arabs, and Providence has favoured them with being settled in areas large and rich enough to ensure their progressive development.

'Let the 400,000 Jews or so withdraw from Palestine and it will fall back to its pre-war conditions. A corroboration is the state of Trans-Jordan and of such districts as Nablus, in which Jews have not been active.

'I know that the Arab leaders will clamour at the top of their voice, "Go! we can do without all your advantages." Were the Jews to go, the first to recall them would be those same leaders, and the entire Arab population.

'That this would be the case can be ascertained from the efforts being made after the strike to force the Jews to return to the use of the Port of Jaffa. The Arabs and their leaders have done the utmost in their power to chase them out from Jaffa town and Jaffa harbour. With the strike over, paradoxical as it may sound, the same seamen and leaders, including the most intransigent ones, are sparing no effort to force the Jews back.'

Eliachar admitted in his Report that the Zionist leaders had made mistakes by ignoring the mentality of the inhabitants, and failing to understand and win over the indigenous population. 'Lacking tradition in statesmanship our leaders failed to guage at its true value the Arab factor in Palestine', he acknowledged.

He went on:

'To these early hours and moods we owe many blunders.

'True, the task before the Jewish leaders was gigantic, and the pressure of persecution in Europe and elsewhere demanded, and continues to demand imperatively, the concentration of all efforts upon the transfer to Palestine of as many Jews as possible in the shortest possible time.

'It is also true that the uncompromising attitude of the Arab leaders rendered futile any tentative efforts at a rapprochement.

'My statement may be unpleasant to the ear of many a Jew. But when I set out to voice my opinion I promised myself to analyse as truly as I could the entire complex of the problem. To admit our mistakes with the intention of correcting them is in itself the best excuse and apology, just as a surgical cut is useful though painful.'

He maintained that the two Semitic cousins could still live together, notwithstanding the past, and that Palestine could be the common fatherland of both people. It was impossible for either to oust the other. He visualised the country developing as a federation, under the aegis of Great Britain, with both Jews and Arabs enjoying complete equality, but with the Arabs recognising the Mandate and accepting the implications of the establishment of a Jewish National Home in Palestine.

In a number of recommendations, he covered in great detail how these ideas of his could be translated into a practical reality.

He ended his paper:

'The attitude at present adopted by the Arab leaders is unflinching and irreconcilable. But I do not lose faith in an ultimate understanding once it becomes clear to them that it is impossible to brush away the Jews and their claim over Palestine.

'In mutual understanding between Arabs and Jews, with the goodwill of Great Britain, lies the solution of all the difficulties of this beloved country of ours. Murder, arson and terror cannot frighten away the British Empire with all their interests in the Holy Land, nor can they move the Jews supremely experienced in every kind of difficulty.

'The Arabs are and will remain in Palestine.

'Jews are returning to Palestine on the strength of sacred international pledges upon which they have staked all their future, and they will not prejudice the Arabs.

'For either community to persist in looking the one upon the other as the enemy to be eliminated or muzzled would only mean continuous warfare with consequent disaster.

'On the other hand, by mutual concessions, Palestine may progress towards cultural and economic leadership in the Near-East. It may form the nucleus around which the union of all Arab States under the guidance of Great Britain could develop.

'The safety of the routes of the British Empire may thus be assured for many generations to come and a great and powerful British Empire is the best safeguard for extended Peace.'

Reading through 'A Jew of Palestine Before the Royal Commission', Elie Eliachar says ruefully now that he erred completely in his assumption that the road to Jewish and Arab joint bliss lay through association with the might of the British Empire.

'Who could have foreseen in 1936', he asks, 'that in less than a decade, the greatest empire in the history of the world should emerge victorious from the Second World War, and yet, despite that victory, should disintegrate, lose dominions and colonies, cease to be the foremost country on the face of the globe? Israeli extremists who glory in war should learn the lesson that military supremacy may not always be the answer. Such Israelis talk of winning this war or that war, of beating the Arabs on one battlefield after another.

'But we have to ask ourselves all the time if there is no answer except war to our problems. If we have to fight to defend our national existence, that is one thing — it is quite another to fight to retain assets gained in other wars. We must look always for a peaceful and progressive solution to the dangers threatening our nationhood and independence.'

He distributed his report as a pamphlet, widely read at the time, not only to members of the Peel Commission, but also among leading Jews and non-Jews in the world. He received very favourable comments from Justice Louis Brandeis, who called it 'your illuminating paper', from Lord Samuel, and from Sir Robert Waley Cohen. One of the people to whom he sent it was Pinhas Rutenberg, founder and head of the Palestine Electric Corporation, a fervent believer in Jewish-Arab cooperation, who was to work closely with Eliachar.

CHAPTER EIGHT

COOPERATION THROUGH COMMERCE AND DEVELOPMENT

Elie Eliachar always believed that one way in which Jews and Arabs could get to understand each other and could learn to co-exist was through cooperation in industrial and commercial ventures designed to bring prosperity to the Middle East. In last resort, the overwhelming challenge facing both nations was how to restore prosperity to the once Fertile Crescent, which had become a barren and inhospitable homeland for all its inhabitants through centuries of wars, erosion, neglect and ill-usage.

One of the greatest Jews in Palestine held the same views — Pinhas Rutenberg. Rutenberg had been the governor of Moscow during Kerensky's short regime in 1917; when the Bolsheviks came to power, he left Russia. An engineer, he obtained a concession from the British Government to harness the falls of the Jordan River below the Sea of Galilee, so as to generate electric power. He established the Palestine Electric Corporation, forerunner of the Israel Electric Corporation; it is no exaggeration to say that his electricity transformed the Holy Land.

Eliachar had become friendly with him in the early 'twenties, when Eliachar was head of the Department of Trade and Industry of the Mandatory Government. One of Eliachar's activities which interested Rutenberg considerably was the bringing of Jewish seamen, fishermen and stevedores from Salonika to Palestine. He negotiated with the Arab port workers of Haifa, and convinced them that sharing the work in the port with the Jews would result in greatly increased prosperity. This proved to be correct, and Jews and Arabs worked very amicably together.

A major enterprise inspired by Rutenberg was the creation of the first Jewish civil aviation company. He insisted that Eliachar should become managing director of Palestine Airways Limited, saying, 'This is not going to be a British company, but a Jewish Palestinian one, formed to advance our affairs in the country and the neighbouring countries. This is really the beginning of the realisation of your ideas about the Jews of Palestine integrating in the East.'

Despite numerous obstacles put in their way by the Mandatory Government, Palestine Airways became a reality, carrying passengers, mail and freight. It was given recognised landing rights in Egypt, Beirut, Damascus and Cyprus.

A Meeting with Emir Abdullah
Subsequently, in London, Rutenberg invited Eliachar to attend a meeting with Emir Abdullah, the ruler of Transjordan, the grandfather of the present King Hussein. Others present at the meeting were Lord Samuel, Lord Melchett, and Lord Hirst.

Rutenberg proposed a remarkable venture — the setting up of Jewish and Arab colonies in Transjordan by a company formed with Jewish capital. The idea was to stimulate the economic development of Transjordan, and to bring the two nations closer together for their mutual benefit. The Emir was very enthusiastic.

Incidentally, he told Eliachar that he had seen Eliachar's Report to the Peel Commission and had been very impressed by it.

The daring and imaginative plan never matured, due to the opposition of the British. The official Zionist leaders were also critical of the plan, because Rutenberg had taken the initiative without consulting them.

After Rutenberg's death, his brother, Abraham, also established friendly relations with Emir Abdullah. At one time, in a meeting in Tel-Aviv with David Ben-Gurion, Golda Meir and Moshe Sharett, Abraham Rutenberg urged them to negotiate direct with King Abdullah, and offered to handle negotiations to bring about such a meeting. Ben-Gurion's answer was unequivocal: 'The idea is not desirable, not worth while.'

Much later, when fighting was already taking place, and a savage war in the Middle East was imminent after the British gave up the Mandate, Abraham Rutenberg asked the Emir if he would see Golda Meir and Eliahu Sasson. The King said that he had been assured of victory within ten days by the British, and asked, 'You're too late. Where have you Jews been al lthis time?'

However, a meeting did take place between the Emir and Golda Meir. She has described this meeting at length in her autobiography. But what she did not bring out was the theme, 'You're too late. Where have you Jews been all this time?'

According to Eliachar, this tragic note recurs again and again throughout the history of Palestine and Israel.

CHAPTER NINE

APPEASEMENT IN THE PALACE OF ST. JAMES

The policy of appeasement adopted by Neville Chamberlain's government in its dealings with Hitler and Mussolini in the latter half of the 'thirties extended as well to its handling of the Arab Revolt. The Government's policy was to evade trouble by any means possible. In a classic analysis of the Palestine question, the Peel Commission had ruled that the Mandate was unworkable, that two nations claimed one land, and that Palestine should be partitioned into separate Jewish and Arab states. The Jews accepted the principle of partition, although not the borders suggested by Peel. The Arabs rejected the Peel recommendations out of hand, insisted on a stoppage of the Jewish land purchase and immigration, liquidation of the Mandate and self-government for the whole of Palestine in a few years time — with the Arabs firmly entrenched as a majority. The Government decided to surrender to the Arabs.

The policy was never openly proclaimed. Instead the offer of partition was published in a White Paper in 1937, but nothing was done to bring the Jewish state into existence, as recommended by Lord Peel and his fellow-commissioners. Instead, another commission was appointed, the Woodhead Commission, to investigate if the Peel suggestions could be implemented in reality.

The British Government's aim was really to 'kill' the Peel recommendations, as was proved by the fact that the Woodhead Commission only came to Palestine in April, 1938; it delayed its report until October, more than a year after the Peel offer was made. Woodhead announced bluntly that his Commission had no practical plan to offer; it considered the Peel plan unworkable.

A month later the Government proclaimed that it had given up the partition concept. Shortly afterwards, in December, 1938, Jews and Arabs were invited to come to a Tripartite Conference of British, Jews and Arabs in St. James Palace. The offer to the Arabs included not only Palestinians, but also Arab representatives from countries which were for the most part under British control at the time.

If this Conference had not had such tragic results for so many years, it might have been considered an example of a comic opera. The Arabs refused to sit at the same table with the Jews, so they met separately, with the British attending the separate meetings. Theoretically, the British were functioning as honest brokers: in reality, they were hanging judges, who had prejudged the Zionist experiment, and had sentenced it to death. The Zionists were in good company: Chamberlain had just abandoned Czechoslovakia to Hitler a few months before. The man chosen for the role of executioner of Zionism was Malcolm MacDonald, the Colonial Secretary.

Eliachar was frequently in London, on his own private business and in connection with the affairs of Palestine Airways. He was with Pinhas Rutenberg in the British capital in December, 1938 and January,

1939. They learned all about the British plan to liquidate the Mandate. Eliachar thought that the Jewish leaders should never have agreed to participate at all in the Conference, since he was sure that the British were only looking for a face-saving formula for a betrayal of the commitment under the Mandate to establish the Jewish National Home.

The British Trap

Eliachar comments now, 'I believed that the Jews should not walk into the trap set for them by the British. It is true that the Palestinian Arabs were not united about the Conference. The Supreme Council under Haj Amin el-Husseini objected to the participation in it of Arabs who opposed the Mufti. They were particularly opposed to any appearance by Ragheb Bey Nashashibi's party, "Adifa", which the Mufti had almost destroyed in the years of the riots. Ragheb Bey Nashashibi and Suleiman Tukan of Nablus, among the leaders of "Adifa", had been forced to flee to Egypt. Thousands of the finest Arabs of the country had been driven out of Palestine, and were fugitives in the neighbouring countries. Fakhri Nashashibi alone remained to organise opposition to the Supreme Arab Council. With our help, Fakhri had managed to strengthen the rank and file of "Adifa" considerably.

'Another progressive Arab group was that led by advocate Auni Bey Abdul Hadi, one of the leaders of the Arab Liberation Movement, which fought the Turks, and Mussa Effendi el-Alami, formerly one of the top officials in the Department of Justice of the Mandatory Government, a scholarly man, with an enchanting personality.

'I realised that the war with Germany was by then unavoidable and that many of the leaders of the Arab movements in our country and neighbouring countries favoured the Nazis and Fascists. Chief among the pro-Nazis was Haj Amin el-Husseini himself. Rutenberg asked me to find out the composition of the Arab delegations from our country and from the neighbouring countries, which would participate in the St. James Conference. On my way home from London, at the beginning of January, 1939, I stayed in Egypt for a few days, meeting there with Jewish and Egyptian friends, with Ragheb Bey Nashashibi, Suleiman Tukan, and my childhood friend, Joseph M. Levy, Middle East Correspondent of the "New York Times", as well as the leaders of the Jewish community in Cairo'.

From Cairo, he wrote to Rutenberg, then in London: 'The Egyptian Government has succeeded in binding together all Arab parties in Palestine within the Supreme Arab Council. Through their pressure, Auni Abdul Hadi and Mussa el-Alami have been accepted as members of the Arab delegation invited to go to London to the Conference. In Cairo, two secret meetings have taken place. From my sources, I learned that the Palestinian delegation has been given the green light to take up an extremist stand, as demanded by the Mufti. According to this stand, Palestinian Arab independence should be recognised, and all Jewish immigration should be stopped. The rest of the Arab delegations, meanwhile, will act as intermediaries for compromise. The Jordanians and Iraqis will support, among other things, permitting immigration of not more than ten thousand Jews annually — on condition that the Balfour Declaration is declared null and void, since its purpose — a national home — had been, as it were, realised.

'The Jews should be given representation, relative to their numbers in the country, in a sovereign Palestinian Arab State, which will be bound to Britain, by the same kind of pact as Britain has with Iraq.'

Eliachar was horrified by what was going on, and by the naivete with which the Jewish leaders were plunging ahead into the British trap.

The Fatal Error — Bringing in Other Arab States

'What worried me most was that, for the first time in history, the Jews were recognising the right of the leaders of the surrounding Arab countries to have a say in the future of Palestine. The Balfour Declaration and the Mandate had recognised the link and interdependence of the Jewish National Home and the Jews of the Diaspora. But, while they protected the rights of the Palestinian Arabs, these documents never mentioned the right of countries like Egypt, Syria and Iraq to interfere in the destiny of Palestine. At the St. James Conference, the British for the first time were giving *official* endorsement to such interference. And the Zionist leaders were cooperating.

'The repercussions of this terrible error are affecting us to this day. *Ever since St. James, the Arab leaders of countries outside Palestine have been accorded the right to intervene in the fate of our country.* In fact, by a curious topsy-turvy reasoning, our leaders today seem to *prefer* to deal with alien Arab leaders than with the Palestinian Arabs, the people directly involved. These leaders deny the existence of a Palestinian entity, but assume that Egypt, Jordan,

Syria, Lebanon, Iraq and Saudi Arabia all have views which should be considered.'

In the light of his conviction that the British were planning a gentlemanly stab in the back for the Jews, Eliachar urged Rutenberg again to use his influence to get the Jews to boycott the Conference. Rutenberg was doubtful at first, but eventually agreed that Eliachar was right.

But nothing helped. The Jews sat in one room, the Arabs in another. The British scuttled from room to room. Fine speeches were made. At the thirteenth meeting the British produced their plan.

The MacDonald Plan

The British proposed the setting up of a sovereign Palestinian State, which would be connected with Great Britain, and the creation of economic and military conditions, which would make possible peaceful co-existence of the two peoples. In this way, the existence of the Mandate over Palestine would come to an end.

They emphasised that it was not the intention of His Majesty's Government to turn Palestine into a Jewish State or an Arab State. Nor did the Government see any obligation on its part to advance either of these alternatives. It would be a State in which Jews and Arabs would participate in one government, in a form which would guard the vital interests of each of the two nations. A constitution of a sovereign state would be set up, which would guarantee the rights of the individual, the rights of preservation of all holy places, the protection of the rights of other communities, as well as preservation of the special rights in Palestine, flowing from the existence of the Jewish National Home.

MacDonald's plan laid down that for five years, Jewish immigration would be reduced to a rate which would prevent the Jewish community ever reaching more than a third of all the citizens of the country, that is, one-third Jews as against two-thirds non-Jews. For five years, only 75,000 Jewish immigrants would be permitted to enter the country. After five years, all Jewish immigration would depend on the consent of the Arabs and of the British Government. He went out of his way to stress that his Government had decided to prevent all 'illegal' immigration by Jews. All illegal immigrants would have to be accounted for, and the quota of legal immigrants reduced accordingly. With regard to land purchase, the High Commissioner would be entitled to determine the boundaries for the prohibition of land transfer to Jews.

Although the proposals represented such a craven surrender to extremism by the British, Jamal Effendi el-Husseini, speaking for all the Arab delegates, said that they had to discuss these proposals amongst themselves. He added that the Arabs had already received the proposals ten days before, and had rejected them.

A considerable part in this venomous debate was taken by Christian delegates in the Arab delegation, with George Antonius as their leader. Only Jamal el-Husseini, Antonius, Khaldi and Mussa Bey el-Alami took part in the discussion. The rest of the delegates from the other countries, as well as the moderates among the Palestinians, were satisfied with the announcement of Jamal Husseini that they should rediscuss the proposals among themselves.

Eliachar says,

'Fakhri Nashashibi, whom I met after this meeting, told me that the rest of the Arab delegation were inclined to accept MacDonald's proposals as a first step towards the liquidation of the Jewish National Home. Ragheb Nashashibi and his group were in the minority, although they had access to the other Arab delegations. The proposals would not be accepted, of course, by the Jews, as one could expect — he said — but neither would they be accepted by the Arabs. In view of the danger of imminent war, the discussions would be stopped, and the British Government had already prepared a "White Paper," which would contain the proposals as emergency measures.'

War panic brought about the dispersal of the Conference. There was no summing up, and everybody went home.

MacDonald's 'White Paper' was published. It proved manifestly that the British Government had dishonoured all its obligations, set out in the Balfour Declaration and the Mandate.

CHAPTER TEN

THE U.N. COMMISSION OF INQUIRY

The British Government approved the shameful MacDonald White Paper in 1939: this virtually repudiated the Balfour Declaration and the Mandate over Palestine. It also disregarded all the recommendations of the Peel Commission. The Government announced a virtual end to Jewish immigration and land purchase, and the creation within a few years of an Arab-dominated state.

At the same time, as soon as World War II broke out, strong action was taken at last to suppress the riots. The Mufti Haj Amin el-Husseini went to Berlin, from where he issued pro-Nazi statements. Peace and quiet reigned in Palestine. The Jews, in the words of Ben-Gurion, tried to fight the war against Hitler as if there was no White Paper, and the White Paper as if there was no war. A long struggle to establish a Jewish Brigade was resisted firmly by the British authorities. The Brigade was eventually established as a result of Winston Churchill's personal intervention.

As soon as the War ended, the Jews of Palestine, supported by the Jews of the world, set out to destroy the White Paper. "Little ships', old and rickety, crossed the Mediterranean, bringing the survivors of the Holocaust. Ernest Bevin, the British Foreign Secretary, turned the might of the Royal Navy against them in what Churchill called 'Bevin's squalid war.' Some of the so-called 'illegal immigrants' got through;

others were captured by the Royal Navy and taken once more to concentration camps, this time in Cyprus.

The whole world was outraged. Eventually, under great pressure, particularly from the Americans, Britain agreed to refer the problem to the United Nations. The U.N. sent yet another Commission of Enquiry to Palestine, that much-enquired land. Eliachar gave evidence *in camera* before the Commission, as President of the Sephardi Community, together with First in Zion, Chief Rabbi Ben-Zion M. H. Uziel, and Benjamin Sassoon.

Jews of the Orient

In his evidence Eliachar said:

'We thank you for granting us this hearing *in camera*. Not that we have anything to say that we would not like everybody to know, but for fear that this may endanger the position of our brethren in the Arab countries, as we shall explain further.

'The Sephardi and the Oriental Jews are an integral part of the Jewish People. The differences are those created by different environments, habits and the use of slightly different Prayer Books and rituals.

' "Sephardi" means a descendant of Jews from Spain and Portugal, as against "Ashkenazi", a descendant from Jews of Germany and Central Europe. The denomination "Sephardi" includes all Jews using the same Prayer Books and following the same rituals, which means, therefore, all Jews of the Oriental and Middle Eastern countries.

'In Palestine, with the revival of Hebrew, these differences are gradually disappearing and one Nation, with one religion and the same ideals and aspirations is growing.

'As you were told already, Jews resided in Palestine without interruption ever since the dispersion by the Romans. The most ancient Community is that of the Oriental Jews, who never left Palestine or the Middle Eastern countries, followed by the Spanish Jews, returning here after the expulsion from Spain in 1492. Our Community was organised and has continued to operate uninterruptedly since 1272. We number in Jerusalem over 50,000, and, in Palestine, about 180,000, or over one-quarter of the Jewish population.

'Before the British and Allied Occupation of the Middle East, this entire area was under Turkish rule and domination. This point must be made very clear. Jew and Arab alike were subjected to the iron fist of the Turk. None had any advantage over the other, except the advantages granted by Moslem Law to Moslems over the Infidels.

'Jews of Turkish nationality were allowed to move about freely, to settle everywhere they liked, to buy land wherever they pleased.

'Immigration from outside the Turkish Empire was regulated, but illegal immigration was flourishing. The only difference from present times was that no immigrant was expelled once he had entered Palestine, and no British fleet took Jews to British concentration camps in Cyprus——-with all the ensuing misery and suffering.

'Arab-Jewish relations were good in the social and economic fields. They traded freely together, they met socially, and Jewish schools were attended by the upper classes of the Arabs. I have myself studied with many of the present day Arab leaders of Palestine and abroad, and many are still my best friends.

Judge Louis Brandeis, member of the Supreme Court of the U.S.A.

Supreme Court of the United States
Washington, D.C. Dec. 3, 1937

Dear Mr. Eliachar:

Let me thank you for your illuminating paper.

Cordially,
Louis D. Brandeis

Mr. Elie Eliachar.

Letter from Brandeis

Letter from Lord Samuel

32, PORCHESTER TERRACE, W. 2.
PADDINGTON 0040.

2nd July, 1937.

Dear Mr. Eliachar,

I am very grateful for the letter of congratulation which you were good enough to send me a little while ago. I appreciate greatly the kind observations which you make.

I have delayed answering your letter until I had had an opportunity of reading the pamphlet which you kindly sent me. This I have now done, and with much interest. We are all awaiting with anxiety the recommendations of the Royal Commission.

It was a pleasure to meet you on the occasion of our talk with H.H. The Emir.

Yours sincerely,

Samuel

We were comrades-in-arms during the War, and better friends it is difficult to find.

'Over one million Jews reside in the various Arab or Moslem countries. Their position is one that requires all your attention. Their case has been linked to the Palestine Problem by the force of events and of the acts of their rulers.

'While we deplore the fact that you have not as yet visited the D.P. camps in Europe, which would have explained our problem more than all reports and speeches can do, we believe that you ought also to pay a visit to the Jewish ghettos in the Yemen, in Iraq and in Syria. Only in the D.P. Camps of Europe and these ghettos will you be able to grasp the imminence of the dangers facing our Jewish Brethren in the West as well as in the East.

'It is through you that we are in duty bound to sound the alarm and call upon the human conscience of the world to take stock before it is too late. What has happened under the Nazi regime in the West may happen under the rule of certain governments, members of the United Nations Organisation. Many hundreds of thousands of Jews look up to you, honourable gentlemen, to prevent a repetition of massacres such as those in Baghdad under Rashid Ali, when hundreds were killed, or in Tripolitania under the British Flag of Occupation, where 120 men, women and children were brutally butchered. It is an open secret that the Arab League and the Arab governments consider the Jews in their realms as hostages for the Palestine problem. They have declared this openly. Jew-hatred and Jew-baiting are growing daily in almost all Arab countries. What has happened in Baghdad, in Tripolitania, Urfa, in Egypt, may happen again and elsewhere with increased violence.

'So-called democratic countries, members of the UNO sitting with you, are indulging in racial discrimination bearing the seeds of unrest.

'Gradually and methodically the Jews in Iraq, in Syria, in Lebanon, in Egypt, are being subjected to a special treatment which is enforced administratively but cannot be traced in legal documentation.

'Threats to individuals are daily occurrences.

'A straight-jacket is tightening on Jews there in their economic life. Any Jewish-Hebrew culture is objected to. Any connection with Jewish Palestine is discouraged. Obstacles and difficulties are placed in the way of all Jews desirous to visit Palestine for any reason. Passports are marked "not valid for Palestine". All Iraqi Jews *are held prisoners* and may seldom leave Iraq, only against heavy cash deposits. Jews of all nationalities — American, British or any other — cannot cross Iraq even in transit, and no transit visas are granted to Jews by member states of the Arab League, except under great pressure. Recently all transit of goods to Iraq via Palestine has been officially prohibited, so as to tighten the boycott against Palestine Jews.

'Racial economic boycott, supposed to be condemned by the Atlantic Charter, is openly declared and enforced by all Arab States against Jewish Palestine. Notices to this effect can be seen exhibited at certain customs stations. It is a continual cause of amazement that this continues to be tolerated to this day by the Mandatory, who is supposed to protect our interests, and by the United Nations, which has accepted the Four Freedoms.

'Heavy penalties are imposed upon Jews trying to

leave Syria for Palestine, and, should any succeed in escaping, his relatives left behind are persecuted and imprisoned. That this anti-Jewish campaign has reached alarming proportions is evidenced by the recent broadcasts of Premier Nokrachi of Egypt and Dr. Regheb Pake, Premier of Turkey, appealing to their peoples for moderation. We have referred to Iraq, Syria and Egypt. Conditions in the Yemen, Afghanistan, Tripolitania and elsewhere are incomparably worse . . .

'Conditions in Morocco, Algeria, in Tunis, are now deteriorating due to anti-French feelings running high and, as usual, the Jew is first to suffer. In many countries, such as Egypt, xenophobia is the basis of all these events and moods, but the Jews — the usual scapegoats — with no Power to back them, shall pay for the lot.

'Religious fanaticism, coupled with national chauvinism and mass ignorance are fraught with dangers, particularly since an anti-Jewish campaign is kept ablaze everywhere under anti-Zionist pretences.

'Since the Jewish communities in all the countries referred to cannot come forward and make their own statements to you, we are entitled to speak for them because of our direct connection and kinship as well as our relative security. Furthermore, the presence of His Eminence, the Chief Rabbi — the recognised highest religious authority of Sephardi Jewry throughout the world, as his title "First in Zion" denotes — may suffice to bear evidence of our grave forebodings. Our numbers in Palestine are gradually and regularly increasing by immigration from those countries in the face of all obstacles, dangers and risks for the immigrants themselves and for their relatives and friends remaining behind. Suffice it to note that the Community of Damascus, which numbered about 20,000 before World War I, now numbers not more than 2,000 souls; most of them have reached Palestine. Another illustration is the "illegal" boat, among so many illegal boats, "Yehuda Halevi" carrying over 350 immigrants from North Africa. This is not propaganda. No human being who is free and enjoying a modicum of security would willingly accept all the hardships entailed and the certitude of ending in a concentration camp in Cyprus unless his future, nay, his life — is in danger. It is the result of what happened in Tripolitania and of what everyone of us fears is in store for our brethren in the countries referred to.

'Having been born in Oriental countries, knowing their customs and languages, their modes of life and their ethics, the Sephardim are called upon to play a greater role in the establishment of harmony and peace throughout the Middle Eastern countries, provided the United Nations Organisation is strong enough to impose upon all their members enforcement of the tenets of real and true democracy, the tenents of the Atlantic Charter and the Four Freedoms.

'Most of the Arab countries with the exception of Egypt, are under-populated. No Arab country is in a position alone to put to good use the extensive areas allocated to them so very generously by the victors of the First World War.

'It is high time that the wrongs done to Judaism in the West be somewhat repaired by the assistance required to establish a Haven of Refuge for them in their National and Historic cradle. The more so, before more and irreparable wrong is done to the Jews of the East by the Arab rulers.

'For these and many more reasons given to you by the official spokesmen of the Jewish People, it is imperative that the Gates of Palestine be thrown open to receive not only those who escaped the Hitlerite crematoria, but also those in imminent danger in certain countries of the Middle East. Oriental Jewish Immigration into Palestine will not alter the numbers of Jews in the Middle East...

'Summarising the picture, we now see that with the tacit consent of the governments that could prevent it, men such as the Mufti in Cairo, Yunis El Bahri in Transjordan, Rashid Ali in Baghdad, Anton Saade in the Lebanon, Kawkaji in Syria, Drause in Damascus, are helping to shape the future. Does it surprise you, honorable gentlemen, that we are worried?

'As the indigenous Jewish population of Palestine, we demand the restitution of our rights, by the abolition of the White Paper of 1939 and all it stands for, and the Opening of the Gates to all those Jews in need of a HOME, whether from East or West.

'Not wanted anywhere — undesirable everywhere — the germ of restlessness and despair is eating up in us, root and branch.

'To impose upon Palestine a permanent Jewish minority is to add insult to injury. Knowing what we have to expect under Arab rule, we cannot but declare to you that one and all we shall be faced with Samson's desperation.

'The courageous establishment of a haven of refuge for the most persecuted People since Man was created — may bring peace to this country, to the Middle East and to the world, in collaboration with all our Semite and Arab brethren...'

CHAPTER ELEVEN

JEWS IN ARAB LANDS

Arab leaders have circulated many myths in the propaganda war waged between them and the Zionists for several decades. It may well be that themselves have come to believe some of these legends.

Thus they contend that Jews living under Arab dominion were always well treated; that the concept of the Jewish National Home, and the creation of the State of Israel, were solutions to a European problem that had nothing to do with the Middle East; that almost all the Israelis are aliens injected into a region from which they should be ejected and returned to the Europe of their birth; that it would be possible to create a Palestinian Arab state, replacing Israel, in which a Jewish minority could live in equality, liberty and harmony under Arab hegemony.

Eliachar claims that the experience of Jews in Arab lands was similar to that of Jewish minorities in most countries in the world; sometimes they were treated well, sometimes they were subjected to disabilities, sometimes oppression took the form of physical persecution. Many Jews exposed to the mercies of Arab majorities have suffered murders, rape and pillage in much the same way as did the European communities in pre-Hitler days, although these attacks never reached the climax of the auto-da-fé of the Inquisition or the supreme horror of systematic annihilation introduced by the Nazis. On the other hand, he says that at certain periods the Jews made phenomenal progress under Arab and Turkish rule. Their social, cultural, literary and economic contributions to their societies enriched civilisation. Until the emancipation of the eighteenth century, the foremost Jewish writings were composed in Arabic written in Hebrew characters. The interchange of Jewish and Islamic science, philosophy, literature and poetry reached a high peak.

He points out that Jews in the world can be divided roughly into two categories, the Ashkenazis and the Sephardis. Most of the Ashkenazis came from Europe and their mother tongue, or that of their ancestors, was Yiddish. The Sephardis descend from the Jews of Spain and those who lived in Oriental countries, speaking Judeo-Spanish and Arabic.

He says that for countless centuries Sephardi Jews had lived in Palestine, Egypt, Iraq, Syria, Lebanon, Yemen, Morocco, Libya and other lands in the Middle East and North Africa. For that matter, he adds, there were some Ashkenazi families that lived in these countries for generations.

These Jews were used as pawns in a political struggle, just as Jews have been used everywhere. When the U.N. resolution of November 29, 1947, was passed, terrible pogroms broke out in Iraq, Aden, Syria, Egypt and Lebanon. Over 500 Jews were killed in a single night. Riotous mobs, encouraged by their governments, attacked Jews in several countries. Even a community as far away as Afghanistan was attacked. Subsequently, the Jews of Urfa were victims of equally ferocious pogroms.

When news of the sufferings of the Jews of the Orient reached Palestine, the leaders were caught on the horns of a terrible dilemma. They were pressing for the immediate independence of the Jewish State; the price for this demand was being paid by the Sephardi communities at the mercy of the Arabs.

The agonising Sephardi communities appealed to Eliachar as their leader to do all in his power to save the persecuted Jews in Arab lands. The Jewish Agency, the Va'ad Leumi and David Ben-Gurion supported that appeal. He went to France, England and the U.S.A. He found that British leaders were either hostile or indifferent; the Americans were sympathetic; the French were genuinely helpful. The French aid took practical form: they took real action to protect Jewish minorities in lands that at that time were part of the French Empire or subject to French influence.

Eventually, after years of strenuous efforts, most of the Jews of the Orient were allowed to emigrate from the Arab lands, although, in some countries, like Syria, they are still being held, virtually as captives. Most of the Jews who left the Arab countries came to Israel, but they were stripped of all their possessions, and arrived penniless in the Jewish Homeland.

Eliachar believes that the Arabs released the Jews for several reasons. They wanted to get rid of a section of the population they no longer trusted because it had been alienated by ill-treatment; Arabs in government or close to it wanted to acquire Jewish property; they hoped that the influx of hundreds of thousands of destitute Jews would prove to be an intolerable burden for Israel.

For years these Jews did in fact suffer great hardships in Israel, and the young state had difficulty in absorbing them. But, like all immigrants, when given a chance, they proved to be great economic assets, not burdens.

'About 800,000 Sephardi Jews immigrated to Israel, and today they form a majority of the population,' says Eliachar. 'This disposes once and for all of the argument that the Israelis are all former Europeans wished on a reluctant Middle East by conscience-stricken European leaders, trying to give the survivors of the Holocaust some form of compensation at Arab expense, outside the continent of Europe. Since so many Israelis are indigenous to the area, the whole argument is fallacious.

'I always maintain', says Eliachar, 'That our own government failed to impress on the conscience of the world the terrible wrongs done to the Jews in Arab lands. The Arabs were very skilful in describing the plight of the Arab refugees, with their property left behind in Israel. But we should also have hammered away, over and over again, on the deprivations our Jewish refugees from Arab countries suffered, and the loss by them of billions of dollars worth of property.'

Since 1949 he has raised these points many times. Foreign Ministers Abba Eban and Yigal Allon both claimed in letters to him that they had frequently argued that the losses inflicted on the Jews in Arab lands offset the losses suffered by the Arabs who left Israel under orders to do so from their leaders, and not because of Israeli pressure. But Eliachar is still not satisfied that the argument has been advanced with sufficient vigour to impress itself on mankind.

His claim from the political angle was that there has been an exchange of populations in the region, either forced by circumstances or provoked by the Arab leaders, which has resulted in some Arabs leaving their homes in Palestine in 1948 as against Jews being forced by Arab persecution to seek refuge in Israel. 'Incidentally,' he points out, 'a remarkable fact about this exchange is that the numbers on the two sides are almost equal.

'Furthermore, nobody can claim that the Jewish refugees who came to Israel from Arab lands are strangers to the Middle East, so the argument of people like Yasser Arafat that they should "return to Europe" is completely fallacious. They were, and are, part and parcel of the ethnic elements of this area; in fact, many of their families lived in the lands that have become the independent Arab countries for far longer periods than the Arabs themselves. For over 2,000 years these Jews have been a Middle East people.

'So the majority of Israelis are Middle Eastern in origin. This historic occurrence could provide a good basis for an understanding between the Jews and the Arabs, once both sides accept that the Jews are not an alien European element in the region. Unfortunately, the Israeli authorities have continuously rejected this thesis on flimsy and sometimes objectionable grounds.'

Ben-Gurion insisted to Eliachar that all Israelis coming to Israel, irrespective of their origins or reasons for emigration from the lands in which they had lived, were 'olim' — meaning that they were 'going up to the Jewish Homeland' — and should not be regarded as refugees. Eliachar concedes that this is true for all internal Israeli and Jewish purposes, both practical and spiritual. But the principle that immigration to Israel is an 'ascent' in life is no reason for refusing to use their anguish to counter the claims of the Arabs that only the Palestinians are refugees in the Middle East. 'Underlying the Ashkenazi objections to using the argument about the Jews being part of the Middle East', says Eliachar, 'is the subconscious reluctance to declare that Israel has a Levantine Jewish majority.'

Token Recognition of Principle

Under pressure from Eliachar, some references were made to the claim that there had been exchanges of populations. Abba Eban made the point briefly and half-heartedly in his orations at the United Nations. When Yigal Allon took over the Foreign Ministry, he too used the argument, but also only incidentally and without conviction. Nevertheless, at the request of a few members of his party, Allon did help to establish an organisation 'to demand compensation for the property left in Arab lands by Jewish refugees.'

In 1975 the Ministry of Foreign Affairs organised a conference of Jews from Arab lands to raise the question of compensation, but it was not encouraged to claim that there had been a population exchange in the Middle East. In effect, Israel leaders have tacitly accepted Arafat's thesis that most Israelis came from Europe, which is not true.

Ever since that conference in Paris, Sephardi 'Uncle Toms', as Eliachar calls them, have stressed the financial problem caused by the expulsion of the Jews, instead of stressing the moral and political aspects. To make such financial claims, he points out, it was hardly necessary to create a new organisation; the World Sephardi Federation already existed, and could have been the ideal spokesman for the Jews of the Orient, if its leaders had been allowed to act independently in these matters.

'What was needed,' asserts Eliachar, 'was the appointment of Sephardi Jews to Israel's delegations to the U.N., men who could say that they themselves had been turned by Arab persecution into destitute and homeless refugees. There is all the difference between Eban or Allon making speeches, however good, about people, and people standing up and saying, "Look at us. Look how we have suffered." The Arabs understand this distinction very well, and never hesitate to use Palestinians as spokesmen whenever possible. As against this, the Ashkenazis in power always insisted that members of the Israeli delegation — all Ashkenazis — were selected on merit, thus adding insult to injury, because of the incorrect implication that the Sephardis could not produce men or women of the necessary calibre.'

Convinced that he was right, Eliachar wrote to the then Prime Minister Yitzhak Rabin, on October 18, 1974, a letter, which said, among other things:

'To my mind, the Government of Israel would do well, to balance Arafat or any other leader of the P.L.O., to send a Jew, who was born, and grew up in an Arab country, and whose ancestors lived there for generations, to appear at the U.N. and state the claim that the majority of the population of the State of Israel constitutes today an inseparable part of the region as a whole, for many generations. In fact there has been an exchange of populations.

'It would be of great psychological value, if a speech were to be heard at the U.N. from an Israeli citizen, who could contend that he had belonged to the region for a period of generations longer than do many of the representatives of the Arab States at the U.N.

'I spoke a great deal about this at my last meeting with the then Prime Minister, Golda Meir, in the presence of the Director of her office, Mr. Mordechai Gazit. I got the impression that she understood that some member of the Oriental community should appear and speak at the Geneva Conference.'

Eliachar received a reply from Mr. Yigal Allon, the Deputy Prime Minister and Foreign Minister, dated November 28, 1974.

'The Prime Minister has handed me your letter of 18.10.74, and asked me to reply to it.

'Your contention about a *de facto* exchange of populations, that is, that the movement of Arabs who fled from the area of Israel is offset by Jewish residents who fled from the Arab States — as well as your comparison between the attitude of the Israeli society on the one hand and of the Arab society on the other hand, to the absorption of refugees who came to them, are fundamentals of Israeli exposition. In tens of speeches and articles, we have raised these arguments, and we continue to do so.

'In my speech at the present U.N. Assembly, the full text of which I am sending you with this letter, I reiterated and stressed these points. You will also find in my remarks at the Assembly, an expression of the recognition by Israel of the existence of a Palestinian entity, and a declaration of our desire for an arrangement that will satisfy the needs of the Palestinians.

'The representative at the U.N. is chosen only and solely according to his ability. And indeed, until now, Israel has been represented with honour at the U.N.'

To this letter Eliachar replied on December 12.

'Many thanks for your letter of 28.11.74, and for being good enough to look through my letter to the Prime Minister, of 18.10.74. I hope you will agree with me that I know all the explanations that have been given in the past, until now, about the *de facto* population exchange, as you say. I also did not miss your maiden speech in Hebrew at the U.N.

'In spite of all these facts, permit me to comment that from all my contacts in Israel and the Diaspora with Jews and non-Jews, including Arabs, the explanations given in the matter, which are, as you say, "among the basics of Israeli exposition on the subject", are not echoed in the mass media of America or Europe. This is not to say that the Foreign Ministry and its Department of Information have not done, and are not doing, their very best in this connection. This is the bugbear. Relying on the amount that was done in the past, is not, to my way of thinking, sufficient, in view of the seriousness of the position, and the many misunderstandings which are causing so many nations to take a stand against us. Of course I take into account all the factors which have caused our isolation: oil, Rabat, the sins of omission since the Six Day War, the Yom Kippur War, etc. I do believe that, in spite of everything, much more can be done, not only at the U.N., but also in the world at large, especially in the non-Jewish world press and through lectures at universities to young critics of ours on the New Left. Suitable action could bring about greater understanding of our position.

'Permit me to express my astonishment at the last paragraph in your letter, that "the representative at the U.N. is chosen only and solely for his abilities".

I do not dispute the ability of those who have represented us at the U.N. until now. My contention was, and is, that in addition to the appropriate representation that we have had until now, it would have been very helpful if Jews of the Oriental communities born in Arab countries appeared now and then. Jews, who were driven out and came to us and settled here in our land, would be realistic proof of our arguments about a population exchange.

'I know without a shadow of a doubt that there is no truth, not even a hint of truth in the implication that there are no personalities among the members of the Sephardi and Oriental communities in Israel, and in the Diaspora, who could not have represented us at the U.N., with honour and with knowledge, just like all those who have appeared thus far. If you think otherwise, I should be very surprised. My point is just that the appearance of a Sephardi Jew could bring influence to bear in a psychological fashion more appreciably than what is said concerning a population exchange to the Arabs in the presence of the rest of the nations. Of course, the power to appoint these representatives lies in the hands of the political parties and the Government. If there are no Sephardis suitable for action, and for this representation, amongst members of the political parties in power, it would certainly be possible to find them outside the ranks of the political parties and the Government. In Israel and in the Diaspora, there are certainly Sephardis, who could fulfil tasks such as these with honour. This, on condition that the establishment does not deny the existence of the problem, which does not make possible any representation of the Sephardis and Oriental community in our institutions, until the new system of district personal elections is accepted.'

Again and again Eliachar urged the authorities to insist on the United Nations giving Jewish refugees from Arab countries the same consideration as the international body was giving to Arab refugees from Palestine. He contended that the United Nations should provide funds and power to its agencies to help these Jews. Apart from easing the sufferings of the destitute immigrants into Israel from these Oriental lands, my proposals would have established right away the fact that an exchange of populations had taken place.

Eliachar's proposals were never acted upon.

Lord Samuel

Emir Abdallah, King of Transjordan, said to Jewish leaders in 1948, when they tried to negotiate a peaceful solution to the Palestine problem, 'You're too late. Where have you Jews been all this time?'

Pinhas Rutenberg, creator of the Palestine Electric Corporation, agreed with Elie Eliachar that Jewish leaders made a fatal error in 1939 when they agreed to let leaders of neighbouring Arab states have a say in the future of Palestine

THE FEDERAL COUNCIL
OF THE
CHURCHES OF CHRIST IN AMERICA
297 FOURTH AVENUE, NEW YORK 10, N. Y.

CHARLES P. TAFT,
PRESIDENT
BISHOP JOHN S. STAMM,
VICE-PRESIDENT
HARPER SIBLEY,
TREASURER

REV. SAMUEL McCREA CAVERT,
GENERAL SECRETARY
REV. ROSWELL P. BARNES.
REV. J. QUINTER MILLER,
ASSOCIATE GENERAL SECRETARIES

April 2, 1948

Mr. E. Eliachar
155 East 77th Street
New York City

My dear Mr. Eliachar:

This is a brief note to report that, following our conversation at my office, I have conferred with Rt. Rev. Henry Knox Sherrill, Presiding Bishop of the Protestant Episcopal Church. He has promised to write informally to the Archbishop of Canterbury, reporting the general substance of our conversation and inquiring whether the Archbishop sees steps that can be wisely taken in England. As soon as I have any further word as to the outcome of Bishop Sherrill's correspondence with the Archbishop, I shall be glad to let you know.

Sincerely yours,

Samuel McCrea Cavert
General Secretary

SMC AS

ראש הממשלה

ירושלים, י"ח בסיון תשכ"ז
26 ביוני 1967

לכבוד
מר א. אלישר
נשיא ועד עדת הספרדים בירושלים
ת.ד. 10
ירושלים.

מר אלישר הנכבד,

רב תודות לך על מכתבך. קראתיו בעניין רב.

כידוע לך אנו יושבים כרגע על מדוכה זו ודנים מה הן הדרכים הטובות ביותר להבטיח את שלומנו וגבולנו. הצעותיך עולות בקנה אחד עם אחד הפתרונות האפשריים לבעיות אלו, ואנו בודקים אותן לעומקן.

ודאי ידוע לך כי אנו מקיימים קשרים עם הנכבדים הערבים מתושבי הגדה ומנסים לראות את מידת חיוניותן של הישויות הפלסטינאית.

ושוב - תודה לך על רעיונותיך ויוזמתך.

בברכה,

לוי אשכול

Letter from Eshkol to Eliachar — In reply to a letter from Eliachar, Eshkol wrote that the Government was trying to ascertain if a Palestinian entity existed. Nothing came of these investigations.

Trucks crossing the Allenby Bridge across the Jordan River

Jewish and Egyptian negotiating teams at kilometre 101 exchange documents

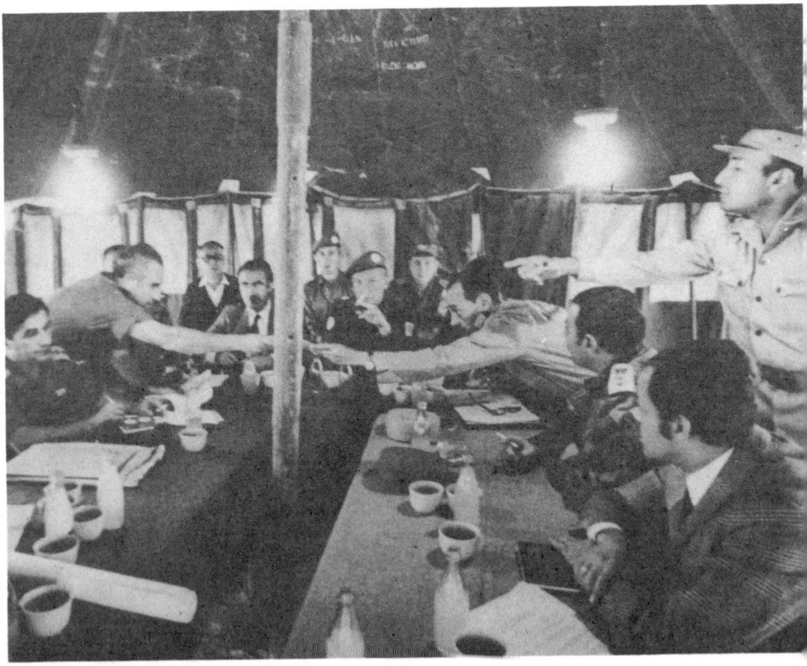

CHAPTER TWELVE

THEY FORGET THEE, O JERUSALEM

The Jews believed that the Christian world would take action to prevent the sacking and destruction of Jewish Jerusalem by the Arabs. This naive and misplaced confidence in the Christian leaders partially explains the utterly inadequate arrangements made for Jewish self-defence in the Holy City. It was then thought that perhaps the Christians did not know or understand the tragedy that was taking place in the holiest of all Christian cities. Rioting Arab youngsters on December 2, 1947, destroyed the Jewish shopping centre known as "The Shama,' including Eliachar's own stores.

While Eliachar was on his mission for the endangered Oriental Jewish communities, he also tried to make contacts with important Christian leaders to activate them on behalf of the Holy City. Some of these efforts were of no avail, some helped.

Among Roman Catholics whom he saw was the representative of the Pope in France, the Apostolic Nuncio Monsignor Angelo Joseph Roncalli, who was later, in 1958, to be elected Pope John XXIII.

'Monsignor Roncalli displayed great erudition about all that was going on in Jerusalem,' says Eliachar. 'He also revealed himself to be a true friend of the Jews, and he expressed his sorrow about all our sufferings at the hands of the Nazis. He accepted a memorandum from me, which he passed on to Pope Pius XII.

But nothing helped. The Vatican adopted a hostile attitude to the Jews, and openly sympathised with the Arabs. Eliachar believes that the Catholic leaders were fearful of anti-Christian action throughout the Moslem countries.

He had somewhat more success with a few of the Protestant leaders. The attitude of the then Archbishop of York was notorious: he did not appear to mind what the Arabs did to the Jews or to Jerusalem. But the Archbishop of Canterbury was more sympathetic.

In the U.S.A., Eliachar went with Bishop Trexler to see Dr. Samuel McCrea Cavert, the General Secretary of the Federal Council of the Churches of Christ in America.

'At first he was afraid that I was trying to exploit the Christian Church for the benefit of Zionism,' says Eliachar. 'To his mind, the Christian Church had to keep outside the political quarrels between the Jews and Arabs. When he was satisfied that we only wanted action to protect Jerusalem from being destroyed, he agreed to help. As a result, the Rev. Henry Knox Sherrill, Presiding Bishop of the Protestant Episcopal Church, wrote to the Archbishop of Canterbury, asking him to use his influence to prevent bloodshed and loss of life in Jerusalem. The Archbishop then issued his famous call for the avoidance of bloodshed in Jerusalem.'

In practice, this proved to be of no avail. For the most part, the Christians of the world remained indifferent to the agony of Jerusalem, just as they were later to ignore the sufferings of the Maronite Christians in Lebanon.

The discovery by the Jews that the famous oath taken by the Waters of Babylon, never to forget Jerusalem, applied to them only, was to have a profound impact on Israeli politics and diplomacy. Already Israelis had a complex because of the Holocaust, a conviction that nobody would help the Jews if they did not help themselves. When they became convinced that only they would defend Jerusalem, this naturally strengthened a violently emotional and hawkish attitude in discussions about the future of the Holy City. Moreover, between 1948 and 1967, Jews were denied access to the Western Wall and other shrines in the Old City, despite the provisions of the Armistice Agreement between Israel and Jordan.

It is little wonder, therefore, that Jerusalem remains the hardest and most emotionally charged of all issues making a Middle East settlement so difficult to bring about. Nevertheless, Eliachar is convinced that with goodwill on all sides, even this problem can be resolved.

CHAPTER THIRTEEN

INTEGRATION IN THE ORIENT

When Israel concluded armistice agreements with the Arab countries in 1949, at the end of the War of Independence, most of the Jews assumed that these would be followed by the negotiation of peace treaties, and that a new era would follow for the Middle East. These optimistic hopes were doomed to disappointment. The Arabs remained implacably hostile. Fedayeen raiders penetrated Israel from Jordan, Syria and the Gaza Strip, with the blessing of the Arab authorities ruling these lands, to murder Israeli civilians. The Israelis replied with reprisal attacks. The severity of raids and counter-raids increased rapidly, with the number of casualities soaring on both sides.

King Farouk of Egypt was ousted by the Egyptian army officers in 1952, with first Neguib and then Gamal Abd-el Nasser becoming the head of state. When Nasser negotiated an arms deal with Czechoslovakia in 1954, it became apparent that another clash between the Arabs and the Jews was almost inevitable. Nasser also quarrelled with the British and the French; he supplied arms to the rebels against the French in Algeria, and he ordered the British summarily out of Egypt, while he nationalised the Suez Canal. He blockaded the straits of Tiran at Sharm el-Sheikh to prevent Israeli shipping operating from Eilat through the Red Sea.

The tension generated by these developments and

the pattern of fedayeen raid and Israeli counter-attack grew worse and worse. In October, 1956, David Ben-Gurion, Israel's Premier, launched the Sinai Campaign, catching Nasser by surprise. In 100 hours the Israeli forces had reached the Suez Canal.

But the Campaign, although it was launched in cooperation with the British and the French, was conducted without the knowledge or approval of the Americans. President Dwight Eisenhower and Secretary of State John Foster Dulles were enraged by the Israeli action, and by the attack launched on the Suez Canal by the British and the French. The American leaders put overwhelming pressure on Israel to withdraw, and, within 100 days, Israel was back in the pre-Campaign borders.

But Ben-Gurion had made some significant gains. He had been given verbal assurances by President Nasser through the Americans that the straits of Tiran would remain open to Israeli shipping, the Sinai Desert would be a demilitarized zone, and fedayeen would not be allowed to operate from the Gaza Strip. And indeed, in the event, for ten years these assurances were honoured.

After the Sinai Campaign

During the years that followed the Sinai Campaign, Eliachar continued to fight for two cardinal principles of his philosophy: the full absorption of the Jews from Oriental lands into the society of Israel, and recognition of the need for Israel to accept that it must become part of the Levant, must acknowledge that its future lay in cooperation with the other lands of the Middle East.

He wrote in one article: 'Israeli cabinet ministers make speeches that are irresponsible and harmful, as if we were not living in a region in which there are millions upon millions of Arabs, as if there are other peoples outside the region to whom we should link our future. Such speeches may seem to be good tactics for the time being, since the Arabs for their part are opposed to peace with Israel. But we must seek all the time for ways to make contacts with them.

'Pinhas Sapir, one of our most prominent leaders, told Eric Rouleau, of "Le Monde": "Israel belongs to Europe, culturally, politically, and economically, in spite of the fact that geographically it is situated in the Middle East..." Moshe Dayan said to the same journalist, that he does not believe in what is called "integrating Israel into the Arab world." He said, "The Arabs do not have much to teach us. Israel is undoubtedly nearer to Europe from the economic, political and cultural points of view..."

'Such speeches run counter to all our words about striving for peace. About this sort of thing it can be said that silence is golden. These two important men and others no less responsible than they, do not know, it seems, that Arab states have people who can read and hear what is written and said in Israel about Israel and the Arabs.

'These speeches provide valuable material for their propaganda, and are used to justify their contention that our state and its citizens are a foreign element in the region, endangering them and their future. These words are used to justify their claim that we do not want peace, that our intention is to integrate with Europe, as though we are seeking connections with Neo-Colonialists, and Neo-Imperialists against them.

'More than this. Neither Pinhas Sapir nor Moshe Dayan can ignore the fact that more than half of the Jewish population, in addition to the Arab citizens of Israel, are from this region, and did not come from the continents of Europe and America.

'My words must not be interpreted as meaning that we should give up all that is good in science, technology, and Western culture. The West can supply much to our state. We need these benefits so as to remain among the advanced nations of the region. For that matter, the Arab nations around us are sparing no effort to acquire Western tools of science and technology. Like us, they are seeking the good in the civilization of the West. We have been given a golden opportunity to serve as a bridge between the culture of the West and the culture of the East, which we inherited from our forefathers. But we are neglecting this heritage in a sinful fashion, in view of our geo-physical and geo-political positions.

'It is the duty of the Jews from the Arab lands, even more than it is the responsibility of their brothers from Eastern Europe, to realise the importance of our serving as such a bridge. These Jews constitute a majority of the inhabitants of this country. It is their duty to influence Israeli foreign policy and social policy, so that we can move towards our true destiny, integration in our region, while retaining our own Jewish culture and our connections with the culture of the West.'

CHAPTER FOURTEEN

AFTER THE SIX DAY WAR

After Gamal Abd-el Nasser, President of Egypt, ordered the U.N. Emergency Forces out of the Gaza Strip and Sharm-el Sheikh, and poured troops into the Sinai Desert in May-June, 1967, another war between Israel and Egypt became inevitable. Syria and Jordan joined Nasser to put a noose around Israel. For some anxious weeks it seemed that the Jewish State was in great danger of being annihilated. Then, in six dramatic days, the Israel Defence Forces routed all the Arab armies, and occupied the Sinai Desert in the South, the Golan Heights in the North, and the West Bank of the Jordan River to the East. Jerusalem was re-united.

This escape from peril to overwhelming victory in so short a time was an intoxicating experience for most Israelis. Eliachar took a more sober view. On June 18, 1967, while the victory celebrations were at their height, he wrote a letter to Prime Minister Levi Eshkol, in which he pointed out that the core of the problem was how to obtain peace, not only in the immediate future, but also in the more remote future. This involved deciding how to deal with the question of the Palestinian refugees. He went on, 'As a result of the occupation of the West Bank and the Gaza Strip, more than half these refugees have now come under Israeli control. The dictates of the moment are to exploit quickly the chance given to us by Providence, and to seek ways of solving the Arab refugee problem. I have already suggested that we should help to set up a Palestinian entity, which can negotiate with our Government, and can represent the Palestinian Arabs in a way that will lead to self-determination for them, and cooperation between them and the authorities of the Jewish State.'

Prime Minister Levi Eshkol answered, in a letter on June 26, 1967, 'Your proposals coincide with one of the possible solutions of the problem which we are now examining in depth. You certainly know that we are maintaining contacts with Arab notables, residents of the West Bank, and are trying to ascertain the extent to which a Palestinian entity exists.'

Eliachar had many talks with both Israeli Arabs and Arabs on the West Bank, whom he had known well in the old pre-1948 days, and whom he had not seen for 19 years. He found that these Palestinian leaders wanted very much to shake off the control of the Arab states: they felt that they had been exploited shamelessly for years. They were ripe to enter into any imaginative scheme for cooperation that Israel might suggest. He reported accordingly to Prime Minister Eshkol and other cabinet ministers.

Unfortunately, most Israelis were so jubilant about their great victory that they talked arrogantly as conquerors. On June 20, 1967, Eliachar wrote an article, entitled, 'Rejoice Not When Your Enemy Falleth...' (Proverbs, 24, 17), appealing for more sober counsels and behaviour.

'After things calm down, and people have absorbed the fact of the victory, we must look sensibly around us, and must draw appropriate conclusions. A hard struggle still lies ahead of the nation. Victory on the battlefield must lead to victory in peace, on the political front.

'It is the duty of the Government, of the leaders of every party and trend, to instil a spirit of humility in the spokesmen of Israel everywhere. Arrogance breeds hatred; boasting is despicable. "Let another man praise thee..." (Proverbs 27, 2).

'We must thank Heaven that friends and enemies alike have been amazed and impressed by the achievements of our sons in a few hours. But these achievements merit our silent appreciation: they should not be used as a trigger for excessive pronouncements by ministers, leaders, Members of the Knesset, and rabbis. Once such pronouncements are made, they cannot be retracted. Victories grow according to the degree of self-control displayed, from the strength of quiet self-confidence, from the determination to end internal differences and seek national integration. We must refrain from running around in search of verbal spoil.

'Our victory has made us behave like people who are intoxicated, like those who dream. But we must sober up, and must give deep thought to our future in the region, to the longed-for peace with our neighbours. Today, they are our enemies. It is our duty to seek ways to turn them into our friends, for the sake of Israel, for the sake of the Arabs, for the sake of peace, for the sake of the progress and development of the region in which we all live.'

Moderate Arabs Ignored
Unfortunately, none of these admonitions were heeded by the Israelis. Even though the Palestinian Arabs in

the territories occupied by Israel gave clear indications that they were interested in cooperation with the Jews, as when the Jerusalem Arabs voted *en masse* in the Jerusalem municipal elections, although abjured not to do so by the Jordanian Government, the 'hawks' prevailed over the 'doves' in Israel. Few leaders gave thought to the danger of not having a long-term Arab policy.

Eliachar says now, 'We missed a golden opportunity in those first few weeks after the victory in the Six Day War. All too soon, the Arabs of the West Bank came to think, with good reason, that we had no real desire to reach an honourable agreement with them. Israeli spokesmen produced plans inconsistent with their professed desire for peace. The Arabs claimed that these leaders really wanted to annex the conquered areas, and were only playing for time to do so when they mouthed peaceful platitudes, on the assumption that time would work in favour of annexation through absorption.

'As the weeks turned into months, the appetite of the "hawks" increased. They came out openly with a claim that a greater Israel should be established, incorporating the West Bank, and the Arabs living there should be given an opportunity to emigrate to other Arab states, of disappearing somewhere or other, somehow or other.

'With regard to negotiating peace with the Arabs, while we said over and over again that we wanted to deal with them directly, with no pre-conditions imposed, in effect we made it clear that we had minimal conditions which they could never accept. The Arab extremists made negotiations virtually impossible — but so did we.'

He pleaded over and over again for Israel to be less obdurate. Israeli leaders said that there were no Arabs with whom they could negotiate; he insisted that they were wrong. Palestinian leaders on the West Bank with whom he talked were very anxious to hold such talks. The only conditions they put to Eliachar was that the Palestine entity and Jerusalem should be discussed separately, a stipulation he considered sensible, since Jerusalem was a special problem, of vital importance to Jews, Christians and Moslems everywhere. His own suggestion was that Jerusalem should be run by a condominium of Jews and Arabs.

All his arguments and pleas to the Israeli leaders fell on deaf ears: they continued to act as if the Arabs would have to submit eventually to the Israeli victors, to make peace on Israeli terms, which would be generous. He continued to insist that this entire concept was mistaken, that Israel's attitude was only stiffening Arab resistance. Even the War of Attrition — the effort of Egypt between the Six Day War and the Yom Kippur War to break Israel's hold of the west side of the Suez Canal, an effort which lasted from 1968 to 1970 — failed to shake Israeli complacency.

In November, 1969, Eliachar wrote an article in 'Bama'aracha', in which he made yet one more appeal for Israelis to negotiate with the moderate Palestinian leadership. He wrote, 'In spite of the growing rigidity among the West-Bank Arabs, influential thinkers and personalities among the Arabs dare to express publicly their desire to discuss matters with us, and even express a willingness to set up a Palestinian entity, linked to the State of Israel in a federal arrangement.'.

He pointed out in his article that President Bourghiba of Tunis had risked the displeasure of the other Arab leaders, accustomed to hate-ridden cliches, when he came out with a sensational statement that the Arabs must accept the fact of Israeli existence, and must negotiate with Israel about the creation of a Palestinian state. A similar view was expressed by Cecil Hourani, a leading Arab writer. All these offers were brushed aside contemptuously by the Israeli authorities.

Then he quoted another Arab writer, Dr. Hamdi Tagi Farouki, who had written a long article in 'New Middle East', in which he expressed the view that the Jews and Palestinians should get together to work out their problems, without the intervention of the Arab states. Farouki argued that the Palestinians had done themselves great harm by handing over their affairs to the leaders of the Arab countries, when they should have concentrated on solving the problem themselves, as a Palestinian problem.

This fitted in with the opinion Eliachar had expressed as early as 1939, when he had objected to the Jewish Agency cooperating with the British when the latter invited leaders of Arab states to attend the St. James Conference. In his 'Ba'Maaracha' article, Eliachar wrote: 'Few Arabs realise, apart from Dr. Farouki — and I doubt whether even one responsible Israeli leader admits it — that a fatal mistake was made by both sides in admitting the newly created Arab states to interfere as partners in our affairs. The main sufferers were the Palestinian Arabs themselves: the refugees, who left their homes first in the War of Independence and then the Six Day War, were the main victims.'

He went on in his article: 'Dr. Farouki maintains

that Israel missed a precious, once in a lifetime, opportunity to make final peace arrangements with the Palestinian Arabs immediately after the proclamation of the cease-fire in June, 1967. I agree with this view.

'Many of my Arab friends from the East and West Banks came to talk to me after the cease-fire. They spoke freely and without any reservation or evasions. They convinced me that Israel's only hope for peace was to negotiate with the Palestinian Arabs. They wanted us to recognise those Arab leaders who had stayed on the West Bank as the temporary representatives of a Palestinian Arab entity, and they said we should also permit them to conduct negotiations with the Palestinians in other Arab countries.

'As we know, this view was not accepted by our government. Since then, the Fedayeen movement has grown to formidable proportions. But, even immediately after the cease-fire, I did not hesitate to accept the stand taken by some of the Arab leaders, who spoke to me about it, that if necessary, the Fedayeen too should be given a part in the negotiations for setting up a Palestinian Arab entity. Why not? The United States longs for negotiations with the Viet-Cong, and France once conducted negotiations with the F.L.N., today the heads of friendly Algeria.

'As a son of this land, I know that, even at the time of the Turks, the Palestinian Arabs were a separate group, very different from the rest of the Arabs in Syria, Egypt, etc. If we look at the past, we must admit that the Arabs who lived in Palestine, form an ethnic group completely different from those formed by other Arabs.'

Golda Thinks Otherwise

He went on to dispute the view expressed by leading Israelis, like Prime Minister Golda Meir and Minister Without Portfolio Israel Galili, that 'The Arabs of Palestine are not an ethnic category, a community with national characteristics, which set it apart... '. According to Eliachar, the Government of Israel was using this analysis to justify its refusal to negotiate with the Palestinian Arabs, or at least to postpone such negotiations.

'Most of our political parties', he wrote, 'agree that the Arabs of the West Bank and the Gaza Strip will remain here, among us. If we continue to deny their nationalist aspirations they will link up with the Israeli Arabs to make one hostile group, persistent and determined, which will threaten our existence. Let us not forget that demography is on the side of the Arabs: their natural increase is far greater than ours. Large-scale Jewish immigration from the affluent communities of the West is a remote prospect.'

He rejected out of hand the argument of the P.L.O. that the Jews were an 'alien branch' in the Middle East region, who should be returned to the Europe whence they had come — he pointed out that the majority of Israelis had come from Arab lands. But, he stressed, this would enable them to serve as a bridge to the Arabs, with whom they had so much in common. The Arabs, he argued, had to accept that there had been a population exchange, and also that the Jews who had come to Zion from Europe had come to stay here forever because of Jewish aspirations through millennia to return here.

Noting that Dr. Farouki described the Jews and Arabs as 'cousins', he maintained that it would be more correct to describe them as 'half-brothers' — Isaac and Ishmael had the same father, Abraham.

'In many respects we share a glorious past. This we have allowed our youth to forget, and it was a gross error that we did so.' Dealing with Golda Meir's argument that the Palestinians had never constituted a separate entity in a separate land prior to 1948, but had merely been inhabitants of a part of a Syrian province forming part of the Ottoman Empire, Eliachar endorsed the view of Paul Johnson, the 'New Statesman' writer (18.7.69), a good friend of Israel, that this was a dangerous argument for Israelis to use, since the basis of their own nationalism might be challenged in precisely the same way.

Eliachar quoted with approval Johnson's argument, 'Mrs. Meir and others do not appreciate the fact that a nation can develop and rise up just because of the pressures of opposition, just as the State of Israel came into existence. Even though the Palestinians perhaps were not a nation, at the time when the colonial nations fixed the boundaries of the region, in arbitrary fashion, according to their own desires and for their own good, today they are a nation. The Six Day War, paradoxical though this is, strengthened, and continues to do so, the process of the establishment of the Palestinian nation.'

Eliachar wrote, 'I mention this article as an example of the thinking of even tried and trusted friends of ours. We must also take into consideration the progress and development of the neighbouring Arab countries, even though their progress is at the pace of the tortoise, since we all know that the tortoise always reaches its goal in the end.

'We must study the economic power of the Arabs,

Yitzhak Rabin, then Chief of Staff, later Prime Minister, in the Church of the Holy Sepulchre, after the capture of Jerusalem in June, 1967, Rabin did not accept Eliachar's argument that Sephardi refugees from Arab lands should be in the Israeli delegation to the U.N.

Prime Minister Levi Eshkol with Elie Eliachar in the Old City of Jerusalem

Sheikh Ali al-Ja'abari, Mayor of Hebron, asked the Israel Government after 1967 to allow him to convene a conference of West Bank leaders. The Government refused

Arabs in Nablus vote in the municipal elections in 1972. Municipal elections were approved by the Israel Government

steadily increasing through the oil wealth they possess, which has partially contributed already to forging a united Arab stand against Israel, and we must look ahead, not only at tomorrow, but at the future of our nation and State in remote years. We must think of generations to come beyond tomorrow.

'I have never believed that we can live by the sword alone, although without doubt Israel must continue to be strong, with a powerful army, in order to prevent catastrophes similar to the Nazi Holocaust.

'But the time has come for us to think of a policy other than that of reliance on military prowess. First of all, it is our duty to walk a little more humbly, we must stop the boasting, quite pointless, of our Prime Minister, of this and that Minister, of many of our journalists. Humility, at the right time and place, will be of great benefit to us. I don't think that Eisenhower or Montgomery boasted morning, noon and night, about their victories over their German enemies. It would be just as well for us to remember that we should not count our chickens before they're hatched.

'All that the Arabs need is one victory. Who can guarantee with certainty that conditions will not change in the future? We have to forget, and help others to forget, that there have been victors and vanquished. We have to look for ways to develop common understanding, and seek for the good in every individual and every nation. Only thus will we succeed in attaining the "Shalom" and "Soulh" (peace) so necessary for all of us.'

CHAPTER FIFTEEN

THE SMUG YEARS

Gamal Abd-el Nasser tried to break the Israeli hold on the Suez Canal by launching the War of Attrition in 1968: this cost many Israeli lives, but the Bar-Lev line held. On the eastern front, the P.L.O. 'Fatah' units, operating from the Jordan, launched terrorist raids on civilian targets close to the Jordan River, in an attempt to smash the spirit of the Israelis in the border towns and villages. These terrorist attacks failed to achieve their purpose.

In September, 1970, some developments took place that greatly strengthened the hands of the Israeli 'hawks', those who believed that Israel must hold what she had, and must not return an inch of the captured territory. The 'Fatah', apparently giving up hope of defeating Israel, challenged the power of King Hussein in Jordan. Hussein, who had permitted them to grow in strength throughout Jordan, turned his strong, disciplined Bedouin army against the Palestinians. In the famous 'Black September' battles, hundreds of Fedayeen were killed, their power to function in military units inside Jordan was broken, and those who survived were forced to flee to Lebanon. Thus the threat to the Israelis living across the border from Jordan almost came to an end. But the raiders went on operating from time to time from Syria and Lebanon.

During the 'Black September' fighting, President Nasser died suddenly, and was succeeded as president of Egypt by Anwar el-Sadat. Nasser had dreamed of one vast Pan-Arab empire headed by Egypt, and had hated Israel for standing in the way of his imperial aspirations. Israelis hoped that Sadat would be less ambitious than Nasser had been, and less able to unite the Arabs in a war against the Jewish State.

Sadat appeared to belie these hopes when he proclaimed that 1972 would be a year of decision, during which Egypt would recover the Suez Canal and the Sinai Desert, either by negotiation or war. Israel rejected his ultimatum. December 31, 1972, passed into the limbo of history without the Egyptians launching Sadat's threatened war of decision. Israeli 'hawks' were exultant; they claimed that the Arabs had come to realise that they could never again challenge the might of the Israel Defence Forces. A spirit of smugness seized the Israeli leaders: they were convinced of their own invincibility.

The main problem preoccupying the Israel security people during this period was that of Arab terrorist attacks on civilian aircraft, backed more and more by international terrorism. The 'Black September' group murdered 11 Israeli athletes at the Munich Olympics in September, 1972; Israeli planes struck back in a reprisal raid on the Palestinian refugee camps in Lebanon. Such terrorism admittedly posed a problem, but nobody considered it a ground for surrendering to Arab demands. If anything, hawkish opinions hardened as a result of it.

After Nasser's death, the passing of Sadat's year of decision without his taking action, and the smashing of 'Fatah' in Jordan, the country's official leaders apparently abandoned all thought of making major concessions to the Palestinians. Moshe Dayan declared bluntly, 'If I had to choose between peace without the areas and the areas without peace, I would choose the areas without peace.' Golda Meir rather myopically could not see that the Palestinians even existed. Even the so-called 'doves' in the Labour Alignment Party, which dominated the Government, 'seemed to sprout feathers like swords', as Eliachar put it in one article. When the Party had to draw up its platform for a general election scheduled for October, 1973, the points of view of 'hawks' and 'doves' were reconciled in a 'hawkish' victory, in what was called the 'Oral Law' drawn up by the Minister Without Portfolio, Israel Galili, a prominent 'hawk' and principal adviser to Golda Meir.

The 'Oral Law' asserted the Jewish right to settle extensively in various parts of the occupied areas, and to hold most of the areas for ever. There was no provision for returning the territories to the Arabs or recognizing the Palestinian entity.

Conviction of Invincibility

The Israeli toughness was rooted in the conviction that Israel was invincible behind the security lines established in June, 1967, and the belief that time was on Israel's side, because the techonolgical gap between Israelis and Arabs was widening. Ultimately, the Israeli leaders were convinced, the Arabs would have the sense to admit the folly of not making peace on Israeli terms.

Eliachar assaulted these assumptions with word

and pen, in private and public speeches, in every way of which he could think. More than ever his role was that of a modern Jeremiah trying to drive sense into the heads of those who did not want to hear. In article after article, he hammered away at the danger he foresaw.

Peace from Strength

In some ways, his positions appeared to be contradictory, because he still insisted that pacifism was not the answer. He had always opposed so-called self-restraint, even in the old days. He still did not believe that a weak or unarmed Israel could survive. But, while insisting that Israel must talk from strength, he also maintained that strength was no substitute for policy.

Thus he wrote during this period:

'The Israel Defence Forces must be ready for action, at all times, under all circumstances, and under all conditions. On the other hand, I do not agree with the assumption that reliance on the power of our army — which today exceeds that of all the Arab armies surrounding us — is the correct way to eradicate for ever the great dangers threatening the existence of our State.

'It is true that the Arab world lags behind in its collective ability to exploit the opportunities made available today by Western technology. The quarrels between the Arabs appear to be so great that they are unlikely to unite in the near future.

'But it is a mistake to assume that such conditions will continue indefinitely. Who can guarantee that the Arabs will not combine in time to come? Our neighbours are advancing with great strides in every branch of education and culture. The number of vocational schools and institutes of higher learning in the Arab world is increasing at a rate that compares favourably even with developments in the most advanced countries...'.

He went on to stress, again and again, the inherent danger posed to Israel by the reliance of the world on Arab oil. This was at a time when both Golda Meir and Moshe Dayan were licking their lips over their joke about the possibility of an Arab oil boycott — 'If the Arabs don't want to sell their oil, what will they do with it? Drink it?' Eliachar took a less witty view of the oil situation. He pointed out that an energy shortage was developing in the U.S.A., which the Arabs could exploit to worsen American relations with Israel. Furthermore, the energy shortage would strengthen the hands of the Russians, and he warned of the nightmare danger of the Arabs deciding to impose an oil boycott.

Demographic Dangers

Eliachar wrote, 'Many dangers lie ahead of us because there are more than a million and a half Arabs in our midst, in the occupied areas and in Israel itself. Their existence and their natural increase could change the character of the Jewish State and bring us instead a mixed State. Such an Israel would mean an end to our dreams. It would involve a revival of an idea favoured by many at one time, that of a bi-national State. It is this concept that the Palestinian leaders of the P.L.O. expound when they say they want to set up a joint Palestinian State for Jews and non-Jews, who will be equal in every respect.

'The fate of India, Pakistan, and Bangladesh, of Greeks and Turks in Cyprus, and of Ireland, all show clearly what dangers can develop for us in a State in which the number of non-Jews steadily increases. I agree with President Benes of Czechoslovakia, who said once, "Kleiner aber meiner" ("Smaller, but mine.").

'We must not ignore the existence of the Palestinians for any length of time, or, in the end, Israeli Arabs and Arabs in the occupied areas will unite to form one political entity.

'Whoever claims that the Palestinian entity does not exist is behaving like an ostrich. It is not sufficient to declare with Moshe Dayan that "Palestine was finished off in 1948."

'It is dangerous to ignore the Palestinians' wish to establish for themselves a recognised state, with national independence, whether separately, or, according to King Hussein's proposal, in the framework of a Jordanian-Palestinian Federation. From time to time, we hear the reactions of moderate Palestinian leaders, about the need to strengthen the independence of the Arabs who live under Israeli rule today, so that they can constitute a bridge between us and the Arabs in other countries. By accepting the Palestinians, we shall bring peace nearer, the peace we all want, the peace that is necessary for them and for us.

'The core of the problem of how we are to live in a region largely Arab, is how we are to reach an understanding with the Palestinians. We can only do this by recognising their existence and by helping them to achieve the self-determination they want so ardently. I visualise a "Palestine" connected with the State of Israel, either as part of a Federation, as King Hussein suggested, or as an independent State.

'Many of our friends are telling us the same kind of thing as I am writing, and we would do well to listen to them. We must use the Israel Defence Forces as a deterrent to defend peace, not as an aggressive tool to preserve conquests.'.

The support for Eliachar's ideas became feebler and feebler as the halcyon summer months of 1973 passed by, with Israelis apparently entrenched in the occupied areas, although in reality they were living in cloud-cuckoo-land. Only a few more thoughtful Israelis agreed with his thinking, among them Arye ('Luva') Eliav, one-time Secretary-General of the Labour Alignment Party, now a maverick, preaching the same conciliatory doctrines as Eliachar. He wrote to Eliachar, 'We broadcast on the same wave-length.' Unfortunately, most Israelis, particularly the leaders, were listening to other channels.

The Unexpected War

On August 20, 1973, Eliachar went to Europe. He left behind him an Israel comfortably convinced that the Arabs would never again dare to challenge Israel's invincible armies standing secure along wonderful defensive lines at the Suez Canal and in the Golan Heights. He found that Israel's friends and foes abroad saw things very differently: they believed that another great test of military strength was imminent, and that war was virtually unavoidable.

He was in Geneva when the Israel Air Force brought down thirteen Syrian Migs. So he rushed back to Jerusalem. Instead of finding the country in a state of anxiety and on the alert, as he had expected, he found that the 'hawks' were more self-satisfied than ever. Everyone ridiculed any talk of another Arab attack, and added that, if the Arabs should indulge in some mad adventure, their armies would be liquidated again, one-two-three.

The Prime Minister, the Minister of Defence, the 'Orientalists', the experts and the interpreters using the media to explain the position to the public, all held the Arabs up to scorn and ridicule.

It was at this time that 'Ha'Aretz' refused to publish Eliachar's article warning of the impending dangers as set out in chapter two of this book. He cried from the heart, 'What could one individual do, going around deep in despair, with nobody prepared to listen to what he had to say, and with the daily press closed to him, in a conspiracy of silence? I was convinced that some tragedy was impending.'

The nation's euphoria came to a traumatic close a few weeks later, when the Egyptians stormed across the Suez Canal, and the Syrian tanks poured over the Golan Heights. The Yom Kippur War had begun.

CHAPTER SIXTEEN

THE YOM KIPPUR WAR

The Yom Kippur War in October, 1973 burst on an Israel unprepared for it psychologically, philosophically and politically, as well as militarily. Only the incredible valour and genius for improvisation of the young Israeli soldiers in the field enabled the Israel Defence Forces to recover from the disasters of the first few days: eventually, from the narrow military point of view, Israel emerged a victor on the battlefields. But, in the larger view of war, she had suffered a resounding defeat.

Her complete dependence on the U.S. had been highlighted by frantic calls for help; without vast quantities of munitions flown across the Atlantic, Israel could not go on fighting, Moshe Dayan admitted in the Knesset. Eliachar's nightmare prophecy of the Arabs uniting some day to use an oil blockade against the industrial world came true: as the Arabs closed the oil tap, Israel saw old friend after old friend turn against her in desperate efforts to placate the oil sheikhs. In justice to these friends, they had been begging the Israeli leaders for years to be less recalcitrant.

The national trauma induced by the War resulted in public clamour for explanations of who had been to blame, what had gone wrong. Heads had to roll. There was much talk of change. A Commission of

Enquiry, headed by Chief Justice Shimon Agranat, was appointed to enquire into the faults in the conduct of the War in the first few critical days.

In fact this Commission unintentionally misled the public. Its terms of reference were extremely narrow, and, in pursuance of them, it sought to find out only which people had been technically to blame for the Army's state of unpreparedness. It censured the Chief of Staff, the general commanding Southern Command, and the Chief of Intelligence.

The trouble with this Commission, as far as the nation learning the lessons of the catastrophe was concerned, was that the excessive concentration on the technical side of war-making ignored the major aspects of mistakes in policy. The implication of the Agranat Commission's findings was that, if only the officers concerned had been more alert, Israel would have scored yet another easy victory.

The Real Culprit

The real culprit in the Yom Kippur War was not this officer or those officers, but the entire philosophy which Golda Meir and Moshe Dayan had preached for years, and had successfully induced a gullible public to accept. This was a philosophical compound of the following thoughts — the Six Day War has proved Israel was invincible; the defence lines along the Suez Canal, the Golan Heights and the Jordan River were impregnable; sooner or later the Arabs would face these unpleasant truths and would make peace on Israeli terms; in the meanwhile Israelis should sit tight where they were, and, incidentally, should imperceptibly absorb into Israel the areas they were occupying. In the result, the Bar-Lev line and the Golan Heights proved to be as 'impregnable' as the Maginot Line.

Eliachar believed for a short while, after the Yom Kippur War ended and there were talks of peace negotiations in Geneva, that the nation would come to its senses and realise the futility of arrogance. All too soon it became apparent, however, that the Israeli leaders had learned nothing, and that they were as convinced as ever that their road was the right one. What is more, it also became clear that they were succeeding in convincing a majority of the people that their line was the correct one.

The first myth fostered on the public was the one that the lines had really been wonderful, despite the fact that they had been breached so easily, because it was only the technical errors that made them vulnerable. The second was to chill the people's blood with the thought — just think what would have happened if Sadat's armies had been close to centres of population, what horrors would have followed! How right we were to insist on holding the Sinai Desert! A third myth was that it was all the fault of the nation as a whole, for going comfortably about its business, and concentrating on trying to raise standards of living and pleasure, instead of practising stern Spartan virtues and preparing for yet another war. Those leaders who had misled the people upbraided them for living high, wide and handsome, conveniently forgetting that the people had merely followed the leader's often repeated advice, 'Another war is impossible — you have never had it so good.'

To Eliachar's surprise, the public, mourning for its dead and lamenting its wounded, in a mood to don ashes and sackcloth, accepted the blame for the follies of its leaders. The new philosophical ideas, really a rehash of those that brought the country to disaster, were swallowed again by almost the entire nation. It was as if the Israelis wanted to accept the blame for the Yom Kippur War, because arguing 'We have sinned', would somehow wipe out the War, and would sweep it under the carpet. Then they could retain the comfortable illusions of the happy period following the Six Day War victory in 1967.

Eliachar was in despair. Nevertheless, he went on talking and writing. Just before the Geneva talks began, he wrote a widely read article pleading for a new approach. In this article he repeated many of his old arguments, giving them a new and topical form. He called his article, 'The Road to Peace: Israel is an Integral Part of the Middle East.'

Illusions Never Die

'The Yom Kippur War should have shattered many of the long-cherished, deep-seated illusions and misconceptions, which guided the behaviour of the overwhelming majority of our political establishment, both in the coalition and the opposition parties in the Knesset. Now, after the event, everyone admits that grave and unforgivable errors were committed, that there were political as well as military errors of judgment, which cost us and our neighbours dearly in terms of human life and material waste. All this would not have taken place had it not been for the arrogance and the ludicrous degree of self-confidence which guided our leaders since June, 1967. From the start, they failed completely to see what was very obvious: that our presence in the area called for understanding and good relations with the Arabs; that we could not indefinitely maintain the existing status quo; that in any war that might be imposed upon us, all parties would emerge as losers.

Israel Must Recognize the Palestinians

'One of the most damaging mistakes made by Israel since the Six Day War has been the consistent refusal to acknowledge the existence of a Palestinian people and a Palestinian national entity, even if, historically speaking, the Palestinians have never before enjoyed sovereignty. It has been wrong to reiterate that there is no distinctive Palestinian entity, that there should not be and cannot be a third state between the shores of the Mediterranean and the desert, and that "Palestine was gone and finished in 1948". It is both historically wrong and morally unacceptable to deny the Palestinian's desire to establish a political identity of their own and a sovereign existence separately, or in some sort of association, with the Kingdom of Jordan.

'This refusal to recognize a Palestinian nationalism is all the more dangerous since, in the last analysis, our success in the search for peace will come only through an understanding with the Palestinians, an understanding which will have to entail extending recognition to them as a people, and, perhaps, even helping them attain the form of self-determination they choose for themselves. My hope is that eventually this will bring some form of federal arrangement with Israel. The fate of the Palestinians in the Arab states, all of whom, with the exception of Jordan, refused to grant the refugees a chance to integrate into their respective societies, did more than anything else to strengthen their national aspirations for a separate existence.

'The refusal on our part to heed world opinion on this and other issues has resulted in Israel's virtual isolation in the international arena and the subsequent hostility of large and significant segments of world public opinion.

Zionism's Original Misconception

'There is historical consistency in this tragic mistake. We Zionists made the blunder of considering the Land of Israel an empty area, an island unto itself. We ignored or despised the millions of human beings around us, the majority of whom are Arabs. A whole assortment of errors have been committed by us in this respect, errors not only vis-à-vis the Arabs who had lived in this country for centuries, but vis-à-vis all those who inhabited it before the Balfour Declaration, including even Jews of the Old Yishuv. These Jews, it is useful to recall, knew how to co-exist with the Arabs, both here and in neighbouring countries. The first waves of immigrants from Central and Eastern Europe brought with them habits and ways of life which included a tendency towards separateness and a sense of exclusiveness, the results of life in ghettos and *shtetels* in their countries of origin. In Palestine, they went on leading a rather closed existence in accordance with the values and mores which had been imposed upon them for centuries past. Pleas made by the old-timers to persuade leaders of the new immigrants of the necessity to establish good neighbourly relations with the local population went unheeded. Balaam's prophecy of some 3,000 years ago was converted into a way of life: "... the people shall dwell alone, and shall not be reckoned among the nations" (Numbers, 23:9). A curse — not a blessing — in my opinion!

'A more grievous mistake has been that over a million Jewish newcomers from the Arab lands who came to Israel after 1948, were similarly neglected as a factor in forging either the character of the new State or the policies which it adopted towards its Arab neighbours. Only now do we see how harmful it was not to have given these newcomers an opportunity to help, or even to have a voice in this crucial aspect of our relations with the Arabs. Moreover, through the education which we gave the children of these immigrants, we inculcated the feeling that the Jews who came to Israel did not belong to this part of the world. The claim that though Israel is geographically part of the Middle East, culturally and spiritually she is part of Europe, has been made throughout the years by high-placed Israelis. We still remember the anxiety and the fear expressed by leading Israelis concerning the dangers of "Levantinization" and "Arabization". These premonitions and derogative attitudes have served only to widen the gap between us and our neighbours, in addition to alienating our Sephardic-Oriental citizens.

'A Semitic People in a Middle Eastern Land

'It should be clear that our existence will always be in danger as long as the present outlook remains

General Moshe Dayan, then Minister of Defence, joins the 9th Brigade in triumph at Sharm el-Sheikh during the Sinai Campaign. After the Yom Kippur War, Dayan asked, 'Who could have foreseen the power of oil in politics before the embargo?' Eliachar had warned him of the danger

David Ben-Gurion with Elie Eliachar after the Six Day War in June, 1967. Ben-Gurion said in the Knesset, 'For the sake of peace I would gladly surrender all the areas occupied during the Six Day War...'

Golda Meir with Elie Eliachar. Mrs. Meir declared, 'There is no such thing as a Palestinian nation...' Before the Yom Kippur War she quipped, 'If the Arabs don't want to sell their oil, let them drink it...'

Menahem Begin believes that the West Bank has been 'liberated,' not 'occupied'

Jewish agricultural adviser with Arab farmer

predominant that Israel is, in all but the geographical sense, a part of Europe.

'The Land of Israel is a small part of a region inhabited by a variety of peoples. Most of these are Arabic speaking and have one tradition, one religion, a shared history and a strong will toward unity. Palestine has never been a clearly defined geographical unit; it was and still is a cross-roads between East and West.

'We Jews are a Semitic people, a Middle Eastern people who were expelled from our land many centuries ago. Our return to this land is conditional on our accepting this fact and behaving accordingly, that is, as a Semitic people, one of a large family of peoples, to which the Arabs also belong. This does not mean that we ought to give up the good things we have acquired through our exile in the West. On the contrary, we must continue to acquire all the technology and know-how the West can offer us. Similarly, we must continue our specific Jewish culture and enhance it by what is best in East and West alike.

'There are some very able Sephardi Jews; it would be a great blunder on the government's part not to include them in the current peace talks in Geneva.

'Time to Settle the Palestinian Problem

'Since 1948, and particularly since 1967, Israel has failed to take the initiative in solving the problem of the Arab refugees. This refusal has allowed the Arabs to turn the issue effectively into a cardinal point in their conflict against us. Now the Arab Summit in Rabat has recognized the Palestine Liberation Organization as the sole spokesman of the Palestinian people; we will have to face the issue squarely, either through an agreement with King Hussein or through direct talks with the guerilla organizations as represented by the P.L.O. and its leader, Yasser Arafat.

'So far, Israel has been calling for peace with King Hussein's regime, and neglected the Palestinians. However, who can guarantee that the Palestinians will not manage one day to separate from the Hashemite regime and thus become a separate sovereign entity, even after Israel and Jordan had concluded a peace agreement? We must not forget that King Hussein has solemnly undertaken to grant the Palestinians the right of self-determination.

'*Jerusalem*

'The status of Jerusalem is no doubt going to pose the most difficult problem in any negotiations with the Arab states and the Palestinians. As a Jerusalemite whose family has lived in this country for sixteen generations, I myself feel very strongly regarding Jerusalem. However, even on this thorny issue, near as it is to every Jewish heart, we will have to seek a compromise solution. To be sure, we should oppose very strongly any attempt at internationalization, which would mean that a third party, neither Jewish nor Arab, would be involved in running the affairs of our city. My own position is that Jerusalem should be the shared capital of Israel and the future Palestinian entity (whether separated ffrom or associated with Jordan), whose municipal affairs would be run by two separate city councils united into one supreme body. Such unification could be along the following lines:

a) The Israeli part, including all holy places within the walls, and especially the Jewish Quarter, would be the capital of Israel.

b) The Arab part, including all Moslem holy places, would be managed exclusively by the Arab municipal council.

c) An extraterritorial status would be given to Christian holy places — similar to that granted to foreign embassies — provided they are linked administratively to the Israeli part of the Municipality.

'None of this will be easy; but given a sincere desire for peace and a new, energetic and more flexible leadership, it is possible. It is worth reiterating here what the late David Ben-Gurion, the chief architect of the State, said on the 20th anniversary of Israel's independence: "Would it be possible, I would prefer peace to territories, with the exception of Jerusalem." In a private talk I had with him later, he agreed with me that we ought to seek a compromise even on Jerusalem, provided that it be recognised as the capital of Israel.

The Sons of Shem

'I have faith in our future, in our Land, in the Middle East as our cradle and our chosen region, should we begin to conduct our affairs with wisdom, moderation, humility, tolerance and understanding of our neighbours by establishing good relations with them. We must never again forget that any peace which would guarantee us an honourable existence in relative security is preferable to no-war-and-no-peace, or to another war claiming more sacrifices of life and resulting in the attrition of our strength. Peace reached voluntarily and out of the parties' own free will is far preferable to any peace imposed on us by the Super-Powers. Disengagement of armed forces through mutually agreed upon demilitarized zones patrolled by U.N. Emergency Forces would furnish safeguards for a fairly durable peace, given that these zones could only be ordered evacuated by a Security Council resolution.

'It is unfortunate that until a genuine and real peace is established and disarmament by all concerned in the area is secured and controlled, Zahal — our army of defence — must be ready as a deterrent against attacks upon Israel. I hope that an end will soon be put to the tragic waste of resources that both Arabs and Jews need to help their underprivileged and to develop our region, the common heritage of all the sons of Shem.'.

CHAPTER SEVENTEEN

ARAFAT AT U.N.

The fact that the United Nations Assembly in November 1974, welcomed Yasser Arafat as a hero and recognized the P.L.O. as the official representative of the Palestinian people came as a great shock to the Israeli Government. They had not expected that terrorists could so quietly be given respectability by the world. On the other hand, despite the pleas and warnings of men like Eliachar, they had done nothing during the previous eight years to help more moderate and responsible leaders to become the spokesmen for the Palestinian entity. There were many wise Arab leaders living on the West Bank, men who had been members of King Hussein's cabinet, and who were widely respected by the Palestinians in the West Bank and by those outside the occupation areas. They had appealed to the Israeli authorities to allow them to organize the Palestinians as a national entity but had been refused.*

Refusing to negotiate with the reasonable Palestinian nationalists about anything except municipal matters, was doomed to end in the glorification of

---

* In September, 1977, Dayan, the man who had refused to give the West Bankers self-government except in municipal affairs, brought forth a new plan to give them a fair amount of autonomy. But it was then too late; the damage had been done.

the extremists based in Lebanon. King Hussein of Jordan, the enemy of the P.L.O. until then, and a rival for acceptance as the spokesman for the Palestinians, had to give in and accept the Rabat ruling.

Thus the Israeli official policy of being prepared to negotiate only with Hussein became utterly pointless. As country after country recognized the P.L.O., Israel's international standing slumped. Eventually, Arafat was invited to mount the rostrum at the U.N. amid thunderous applause.

Arafat's Intransigence

Fortunately for Israel he took an intransigent stance, rejecting out of hand the right of the Jewish state to exist, proposing instead that a single state should be established between the Mediterranean and the Jordan River, a state in which Jews, Moslems and Christians would all enjoy equal democratic rights. This proposal repudiated the basic principles of Security Council Resolutions 242 and 338, which laid down that all Middle East countries, including Israel, had the right to exist in peace. Thus Arafat in effect was standing in opposition to all countries that accepted these resolutions as the cornerstone of their policies.

Eliachar felt that the recognition by the world of the P.L.O. had made Israel's position more difficult than ever, but he thought that good could still be salvaged from evil, if only the Government would change its attitudes and would show some vision, some flexibility, some courage.

'Let us not lose hope', he wrote in an article published in December, 1974. 'We must continue to seek a rapprochement with the moderate elements living on the West Bank and Gaza, who can speak for the Palestinians there, provided we announce clearly that we recognize the Palestinian entity.

'What happened at the U.N. must surely compel us to reconsider our ways and to review our principles. We must analyse the reactions of other countries, not only those friendly to us, like the U.S.A., but even those opposed to us, like the U.S.S.R. and Yugoslavia.

'It is clear that we must reject out of hand the P.L.O. proposal to set up a "democratic state" in the whole area of Palestine, in which all citizens will be equal, irrespective of their religion. This Utopian proposal is really an evil plan to destroy the State of Israel. What Arafat is suggesting is the liquidation of a member state of the U.N., established and recognized by the United Nations. If the Organisation yields to pressure from the oil sheikhs and endorses the P.L.O. proposal, the Jews of the world will have no other alternative but to fight for their lives. Such a clash will inevitably lead to a confrontation between the superpowers and perhaps even to a nuclear war that would destroy everything that man has built up throughout history. We must warn the world of the danger of accepting the P.L.O. view.

'On the other hand, I do not agree with our leaders who argue, "You see, we were right, there is nobody with whom we can talk. How can we talk to a man like Arafat, when he does not accept the basic fact, our right to exist?"

'One of our problems is that decisions are left too much to our generals, in and outside the Cabinet. In the nature of things, generals emphasise the "power to hold on to what we've got". Our civilian cabinet ministers have no policy and trail after the generals. We still have not had a clear stand taken on the issue of a Palestinian entity. Once again I stress that we will never attain peace until we recognise the right of the Palestinians to exist as a nation.

'With almost incredible blindness, we missed many opportunities in the past to come to terms with the fact that the Palestinians do exist as a people. We pretended that we wanted to negotiate a settlement with King Hussein. But we never took any real steps, or announced any major concessions. We prevented veteran leaders in the occupied areas from organising nationalist political activity, thereby leaving a vacuum to be filled by the terrorist organisations.

'Even today, late though it is, if we were to make a clear and consistent announcement of a new policy to recognise the Palestinians, both Lebanon and Jordan, anxious to get rid of the terrorist organisations and the burdens of the refugees, will welcome our proposals.'

Eliachar's article, it is worth noting, was written a year before the Palestinians in Lebanon combined with the Moslems to bring chaos to that Arab state.

Announce Recognition

'Peace will come nearer if we announce our recognition of a Palestinian entity. Let the Government and the Knesset declare that we do recognise such an entity, that we are ready to make concessions about territories in exchange for recognition by all the Arabs of the right of the independent State of Israel to exist in secure and guaranteed boundaries. These borders must be underwritten by the Great Powers and the U.N. As against this, we must allow the Palestinians their own state in the areas presently occupied by Israel in 1967, with considerable concessions in respect of some borders by the parties involved.

'Thus we should announce:

a) Recognition of the Palestinian people and its rights to its independence in the areas occupied by Israel in 1967; b) Our desire to have an inclusive settlement, rather than stage-by-stage negotiations, as time is working against peace; c) Without the cooperation of the two super-states, the U.S.A. and the U.S.S.R., peace cannot be guaranteed in the region. Therefore we must set about normalising our relations with the U.S.S.R.; d) We must make a clear and definite condition that there will be no negotiations about abandoning Israel's sovereignty and her right to exist in agreed and secure boundaries, guaranteed by the U.N., and the two major powers.

'By such a clear statement of policy, we shall remove the responsibility for the prolonged wars in the area from our shoulders. We may avoid the erosion of what little support we have left among the nations of the world. And, if the Palestinians and other Arabs react favourably, we may move towards the peace we all need so desperately, Jews and Arabs alike.'

CHAPTER EIGHTEEN

THE LEBANESE AGONY

All through 1976 and through part of 1977 Lebanon was torn by civil war. Some 60,000 people were killed and much valuable property was destroyed before Syria intervened, nominally, in the role of peacemaker. Many Israelis hailed the tragic fate of the once prosperous little neighbour as a boon to Israel, on the grounds that any internecine strike among the Arabs must help the Jews, and that events in Lebanon proved that nobody could expect Israel to deal with the Palestine Liberation Organisation after what the Palestinians had done to their Lebanese hosts.

Elie Eliachar did not agree.

'I think that these views are specious, and are liable to boomerang,' he said. 'Reliance on inter-Arab divisions has always been one of the most dangerous of all our delusions: time and again we have found that these differences disappear suddenly, and we face a united Arab world in war. This happened to us in 1948, 1967 and 1973.

'The civil war in Lebanon will have a profound impact on the future of the area as a whole. What we need is Arab-Jewish peace, not inter-Arab conflict. Conflicts have a tendency to expand and to transcend borders.

'It is worth while to study the historical background of the civil war in the Lebanon. During the

19th century conflicts between various communities, the Moslems, the Druses and the Maronite Christians resulted in the intervention of the Great Powers, particularly France, England and Russia. France was then recognised as protector of Lebanon by the Sublime Porte in Constantinople. An uneasy peace was established, but sparks were left in the apparently dormant ashes of the conflict, and these flared up every now and then into fires.

'After the independence of Lebanon was officially established in 1943, the relations between the Moslems, Christians and Druses seemed to improve. Power was divided between the Christians and Moslems according to a formula, which established that the President should be a Christian, the Prime Minister a Moslem, the Commander-in-Chief of the Army a Christian, and the composition of the parliament fixed in advance so as to give a specific number of representatives to each community.

'This rigid system would obviously pose a potential problem if any community wanted change. The Moslem population was to grow in numbers, and it began to demand a re-allocation of power in accordance with this numerical strength. At the same time, one party in Lebanon pressed strongly for union with Syria.

The Shock of 1958

'The first shock to the complacent belief in the Western world that all was well in so-called "prosperous little Lebanon" came in 1958. Under the popular slogan of a Pan-Arab entity, Gamal Abd-El-Nasser, President of Egypt, first merged Egypt and Syria into the United Arab Republic, and then got the Lebanese Moslems to demand that the Lebanon should join his new republic. To avoid the danger of annexation by the U.A.R. and the disintegration of the Lebanon through civil war, President Shamoun, a Christian, appealed to President Dwight Eisenhower of the U.S.A. for military intervention to secure the integrity and sovereignty of his country.

'On July 14, 1958, ten thousand American marines landed on the beaches of Beirut. This intervention ended for the time being the danger of civil war and annexation by Syria. It is interesting to note that on the same day the Iraqi monarchy under the Hashemites, set up by the British, was terminated by a military coup led by General Abdel-Karim Qassem.

The Americans maintained a military presence in Lebanon until October, 1958. A new president, General Fuad Shihab, also a Christian, then asked the Americans to withdraw, as he was convinced that the integrity of his country was safe.

'But the potential for revolution remained. Leftist elements among the Moslems and the Druse, supported by a few of the Christians, still wanted to change the old order. Above all, there were 150,000 Palestinian refugees living in camps in the Lebanon, and they constituted a constant running sore. Their numbers increased all the time, and jumped sharply after King Hussein of Jordan suppressed the Palestinians in his country in the bloody fighting of September, 1970. This month came to be known among the Palestinians as "Black September."

'The refugees, now numbering some 250,000, were not grateful to their Lebanese hosts for providing them with some sort of sanctuary, they simply transferred their hatred for King Hussein to the Christian leaders of the Lebanon. They sided with Moslems and leftists, the latter backed by Russia.

'The Lebanese authorities were divided among themselves. I personally believe that Prime Minister Karameh, a Moslem, supported the dissidents in their determination to bring about a change in the balance of power.

'A year before Black September, following an appeal for help by the Lebanese Christians, the Arab League negotiated the famous Cairo agreement between the government of Lebanon and the P.L.O. This laid down precisely what armaments the P.L.O. could maintain, and where, for its attacks on Israel. But the P.L.O. never abided by the agreement, particularly after September, 1970. Gradually the Palestinians increased their encroachments on Lebanese jurisdiction. The Lebanese authorities did not have the will or the strength of King Hussein of Jordan; they were divided among themselves, and feared to take any action which would bring about a direct confrontation with the Palestinians. And the leftist elements among the Moslems and the Druse, led by Kamal Jumblatt, saw a strong union with the P.L.O. as their best means of destroying conservative and Christian power in the country.

'The proclaimed objective of the P.L.O. in its intervention in Lebanese internal affairs was to establish a strong base for operations against Israel. As the dissidents challenged the Christian authorities, the Palestinians mounted more and more incursions across the Israeli border. These were effected in defiance of the Lebanese authorities who wanted to maintain the state of comparative peace and co-existence with Israel that had existed since 1948. Reprisals by Israel against terrorist bases in Lebanon naturally became attacks against Lebanon.

Syrian Aims

'These internal stresses in the Lebanon inevitably played into the hands of the Syrian leaders. One of the fundamental questions running through the history of the Middle East for centuries is which power should dominate the Arab world, Syria or Iraq or Egypt.

'This long struggle led to many military conflicts between the Caliphs in Baghdad and the rulers in Damascus, control moving from one side to the other, with occasional interludes when it passed to Egypt.

'The great dream of establishing an Arab hegemony over a vast area was never given up. It took many different aspects. After World War I, the Hashemites thought that they would control Greater Syria, whilst the Iraqis dreamt of establishing the Fertile Crescent.

'The antagonism between Iraq and Syria was always apparent. The British set up King Faisal in Damascus, and his brother Emir Abdullah in Transjordan. But the French had imperial aspirations of their own, and they took over Syria in 1920, expelling Faisal, whom the British made King of Iraq. Thus the seesaw between Damascus and Baghdad goes on and on, with the Great Powers adding their weight from time to time in support of either the Syrian or Iraqi aspirants to dominate the region.

'The dream of Greater Syria revived when the civil war in the Lebanon gave President Assad an excuse to play the role of a big brother forcing the children to play together amicably. His real aim was clear, his kindly intervention was intended to expand the power of Syria. And he achieved this objective.

'It may seem strange that I, considered a supreme dove, should have opposed Israeli non-intervention in Syria. But it seemed to me — and still seems — to be very hazardous for Israel to have tolerated Assad's expansionist aims.

'The Israeli leaders at that time — Rabin, Peres and Allon — hoping that Assad would weaken the P.L.O. — either decided on their own initiative not to oppose the Syrian intervention, or were induced by the Americans to keep quiet. I have no way of establishing who was responsible for this tragic error — for a tragic error it certainly was. Israel should have opposed any intervention by Syria just as it opposed such intervention in Jordan in 1970. Opposition was vital for Israel's long-term security. The Syrians would probably have been deterred by Israel moving a few divisions to the Lebanese border and into the Golan Heights.

"Allowing Assad to turn Lebanon into a Syrian protectorate has posed a grave threat to Israel's security. King Hussein of Jordan, because of Israel's weak attitude, also had to tolerate Assad's move. Although, like Israel, he welcomed Syria's action in weakening, if not destroying, the power of the P.L.O., his enemies since 1970, he certainly did not want a stronger Syria. But American and Israeli acquiescence in Assad's actions placed Hussein in a very awkward position; he could not be the one to oppose what they accepted.

'Thus a major move for the re-creation of greater Syria politically — eventually, no doubt militarily — became a *fait accompli*, with the tacit blessing of Israel and the U.S.A. The independence of Lebanon, with its Christian element and its desire for peace with Israel and unquestioning support for the West, has become a thing of the past.

'Israel did a lot of good and laudable work in opening its borders to the Lebanese Christians and providing them with all kinds of help under the "Good Fence" policy. But this did not counterbalance the harm done by lengthening the lines across which her main enemies can operate against Israel.

'We can learn several lessons from the Lebanese civil war. One is that the Arab states are tired of the Palestinian problem, which posed a threat to Jordan in 1970 and now has brought about the collapse of independent Lebanon. They want the problem to be solved. Another thing that has become manifest is that the Palestinians *do* constitute a separate national entity: after 30 years, they show no signs whatsoever of disappearing or being absorbed by other Arab peoples.

'Internal conditions in Egypt certainly make peace with Israel a desirable objective for President Sadat — he can gain nothing from another war. But he carries the Palestinian problem on his back like Sinbad bore the Old Man of the Sea. Until he gets rid of it, he cannot afford to make peace. Jordan too wants and needs peace, but cannot ignore the Palestinians.

False Solution

'Another lesson of the conflict is that it has proved that there is no possibility of peace between Jews and Arabs coming about through the Utopian suggestions of Arafat and Begin that there should be one country between the Jordan River and the Mediter-

Jewish guests in an Arab village

Watch on the border on the Golan Heights. Elie Eliachar believes that Israel must maintain her military strength and her vigilance

ranean, in which Israeli Jews and Palestinian Arabs are to exist in harmony. This is an absurdity, whether it is postulated as being under Arab hegemony, as Arafat wants, or Jewish, as Begin sees it. Both peoples have to develop their national aspirations separately, the Arabs tied to the Arab world and the Jews to the Jews of the Diaspora. Israel will then remain a haven for all Jews, its *raison d'etre*.

'The Lebanese conflict has proved again what was proved in so many other lands like Ireland, Cyprus, India, Pakistan — two nations of different cultures and faiths, forced into one land must explode, like two atoms fused to make an atomic explosion. Such an explosion may obliterate the Middle East and possibly wreck the world. The answer lies in separation, not fusion — the creation of a Palestinian state apart from a Jewish state. This truth, always there, was confirmed by the tragedy in the Lebanon.

'I must add a reference to the incredible aloofness of the Christian world, from the Pope and other Christian religious heads to g vernments, when they were asked to assist the Christian Community in Lebanon. All turned a deaf ear to such appeals from Christians facing terrible calamities. France's timid offer to help was discouraged by other western leaders.

'The lesson to be derived by Israel is therefore her reliance on her own strength, not on guarantees of any kind, but with the help by friendly powers in providing her with the tools and the means for her survival — not with any foreign non-Israeli soldiers — whilst striving for peace and coexistence — with her neighbours, but deterring their attacks!'

In 1976 and 1977, Israel began secretly to give military aid to the Christian villages in Southern Lebanon, so as to sustain them in their struggle against the P.L.O. forces. The new Government of Israel, headed by Menahem Begin, continued to give this support, but decided not to be surreptitious about it. Begin announced proudly to the world exactly what Israel was doing to save the Maronite Christians from defeat. The reaction of the Western world was one of dismay and indignation, that Israel was interfering in Lebanon and risking a head-on clash with Syria, with the possibility of another major conflict in the Middle East.

Eliachar comments, 'There is no doubt that the humanitarian assistance offered by Israel to our Christian neighbours deserves praise and encouragement. But Begin's announcement that Israel would stand by the Christians shocked President Carter and others because they are more interested in avoiding a major Middle East War than in protecting the Maronite Christians. In fact, they believe — as I do — that Israel can help the Christians most, not by arms, but by peace; if Israel were to accept that the Palestinians have to have a state of their own, there would be no need for them to seek military bases in southern Lebanon, at the expense of the unfortunate inhabitants of that area.'

CHAPTER NINETEEN

BEGIN COMES TO POWER

A political earthquake shook Israel on May 17, 1977. In the general elections, held on that day, the Likud Party, headed by Menahem Begin, former underground leader against the British and an intractable annexationist with regard to the West Bank, became the strongest party in Israel. The Labour Movement, which had run Israel for so many decades, was ousted from power. The Likud stands for a hawkish line in foreign policy and a measure of *laissez-faire* capitalism in economics.

In analysing the causes of the Likud's unexpected victory, Eliachar points out that it is necessary to review what happened in Palestine even before the State was established.

'From the early years of the British Mandate, the Labour parties combined to control every aspect of Jewish life in Palestine. However much they quarrelled among themselves about ideology and principles, in practice they were united about the need for Labour hegemony. This was in accordance with the principle laid down by Ben-Gurion that, in order to advance the ideal of creating a socialist community in Palestine, Labour had to control all the financial tools which the Zionist Movement was using to create the Jewish National Home. He insisted that the Labour parties had to get together to dominate the Zionist Congresses, and the Zionist Movement.

'These aims were achieved without much difficulty. The Labour leaders were mostly professional politicians as compared to the spokesmen of the other major Zionist parties, who were volunteers working for their livelihood in professions and businesses outside the Movement. Thus the competition was between professionals and amateurs; it is not surprising that the amateurs lost. Only parties wise enough to realise what was happening, like the Mizrahi, appointed enough salaried personnel, and achieved a proportionate share of control.

'As a result, Labour came to dominate the development of Jewish Palestine — agricultural settlement; the creation of kevutzot, kibbutzim and moshavim; the Jewish Agency executive — practically every field of development. Whatever private initiative managed to achieve was due to the approach of the British Mandatory regime, which granted full freedom to free enterprise.

'In its drive to retain political power without interruption, the Labour Movement was aided by the principle of proportional representation adopted in all Zionist elections, the organization of the "Yishuv" (the Jewish Community), and, after the State was formed, in the Israeli Knesset elections. In coalitions with small parties, generally the Orthodox parties, Labour remained in power, apparently for ever.

'One good result was that Israel enjoyed a continuity in leadership and consistency of approach which were rare in the Middle East. Almost all countries in the region were wracked by constant and rapid changes, often achieved by violent means.

'The bad result of Labour's hold on power was that it developed a lack of concern about public opinion, a self-assurance verging on arrogance. Furthermore, all power was centralised within the party; change, even inside the movement itself, seemed to be impossible. Many Israelis felt alienated from the country's leaders, but they could think of no way to influence the conduct of the nation's affairs. If this impression of having no representation was felt by the non-party Ashkenazis, the feeling was even more marked among the immigrants from the Oriental lands, who constitute the overwhelming majority of the poor and inarticulate in Israel.

'Although there were 24 non-Ashkenazi members among the 120 members of the 8th Knesset, they made no effort to function as a Sephardi bloc or lobby. The result was that the Sephardi masses began to feel more and more bitter and hopeless. Gradually they became convinced that they could expect no fundamental help from the Establishment or the Labour Party. Furthermore, decades of power led to many instances of corruption among some top Labour personnel, and the scandals led to the population comparing their troubles with the apparent opulence of many of the Labour Party leaders. Since the Likud was the most active political opposition, the deprived turned to it in their despair.

'The population also blamed the Labour leaders for the mistakes of the Yom Kippur War, and for the economic stresses that followed it. The 1973 elections had taken place after that War, but these elections had been called by Golda Meir in the euphoric atmosphere engendered by the calling of the first Geneva Conference. The false optimism this inspired postponed the submission of accounts against the Labour

Party. It soon became clear that the Kissinger deals only provided temporary palliatives.

'The desire to protest was not only widespread among the poor. Middle class civil servants and intellectuals supported a new party headed by Professor Yigael Yadin, called significantly the Democratic Movement for Change. Thus former Labour adherents in blue overalls switched to the Likud, supporters in white collars turned to the D.M.C.

'Although the repudiation of the Labour Party was so overwhelming, the Likud was not given an absolute majority, but had to enter into a coalition with the Orthodox religious parties, just as Labour had had to do in the past. It has to be borne in mind, also, that the Likud is itself a coalition of different parties; its Liberal component is comparatively strong.

'Some of the religious politicians are very hawkish about annexing the West Bank, but others are distinctly dovish and opposed to the thinking of those who want a Greater Israel. This fact is not widely known outside Israel, and there is a tendency to assume that all Orthodox members of the Knesset are annexationists. This is not correct.

'Because of the lack of contact between the electors and the elected, since Israel has no constituency system, it is impossible to say whether the voters cast their ballots the way they did because of internal issues only, or because they supported Begin on foreign policy also. He naturally claims that he has a mandate to introduce his policies in all fields. He even claims to have a complete national "consensus" backing his attitude to the West Bank and Gaza. In the first excitement of victory, he described these territories as "liberated" not occupied, and earned world-wide disapproval. Since then he has been talking in a more moderate style, uses a formula that "there are no pre-conditions, anything can be discussed in negotiations".

'As time passes, the "consensus" is likely to wane, and splits will shake Begin's complacency.'

Eliachar has respect for Menahem Begin as a man, although he disagrees with him so strongly about so many issues.

'His personal style of living is modest, his courtesy and good manners are not at all superficial but spring from his character, his erudition is deep and he knows several languages. It is no wonder that he charmed President Jimmy Carter during their first meeting. He did very well with American journalists, who, aware of his role in the underground during the period of the British Mandate, expected another Arafat striking dramatic terrorist poses.

'But personal qualities like these will not weigh against irrational political policies. When all the cheering about his new image dies down, he will be judged entirely by whether his approach to the great questions of the Middle East is correct.'

The Honeymoon with Carter
'When he first went to see President Carter, most people expected that there would be a major confrontation, a stormy quarrel. Instead there were undoubtedly genuine expressions of mutual esteem. Begin's first appearances as Israel's Premier in the U.S.A. constituted a real personal success. His oratory, good humour and good manners were acclaimed by friend and critic alike.

'But the agreement not to decide any basic issues, not to try to resolve the very real differences between Begin's thinking and Carter's, only papered over the problem. As soon as Secretary of State Cyrus Vance came to the Middle East, the paper split and the cracks became patent once more. On the one hand, Begin went ahead, in the teeth of intense American disapproval, with his policy of setting up new settlements in what he calls the "liberated areas"; the Americans continue to do their best to bring the P.L.O. into the negotiating process in the teeth of Begin's opposition.

American interests
'There is no doubt that the Americans are sincere when they say that the continued existence of Israel is the cornerstone of their Middle East policy. They want Israel to exist in peace, within secure and recognized borders. But this does not mean that they are prepared to give Begin a blank cheque to fill out in whatever way he desires. They certainly will never endorse annexation, overt or covert, of the territories occupied in 1967.

'The price America would have to pay for supporting Israel, if Begin goes blithely ahead with his programme, is a staggering one. America and all her allies are completely dependent on Arab oil. Can the Western world be expected to risk another oil boycott and the wrecking of their economies to please Begin, however effective an orator he may be? There is another danger to the West — in a further Middle East war, the oilfields of some countries hostile to Israel may be destroyed — a calamity with immediate catastrophic consequences for mankind. Does America's traditional friendship for Israel oblige her to put the world into the hazard when Begin insists on his right to differ from Carter?

'Here is one of the rare instances in history where self-interest and a world view of morality coincide. The Western world, the Communist world and the third world all agree that it is utterly immoral for Israel to annex the territories and to subject the Palestinian Arabs living there to what would have to be an imperialist regime. For this Israeli "right" they will not risk their very existence, based on Arab oil.

'Not only oil is at stake — America's role as the leader of the free world is also in the hazard. Begin argues that Israel is a bulwark against communism that America must support to contain Russian advances into the Middle East and Africa. The exact opposite is true: continued American backing for Israel, if Israel remains obstinate and unbending, must strengthen Russian influence in the Arab and African countries.

'Russia's infiltration into the Red Sea shores is a menace to the American freedom of the seas. This can be contained only by Arab countries friendly to America and the West.

'Israel is completely dependent on the moral, economic and military support of the U.S.A. It is suicidal for Begin to push President Carter into a position where they agree that they have completely divergent views, but agree to differ and still remain friends. This formula, so beloved by Begin, is filled with danger for Israel. It invites the Americans — begs them — to say, "Very well, we agree to differ. We must do what we think best in American and Western interests." Can Israel go it alone? The idea is absurd.

'On his visit to Roumania, Begin achieved the same result as he had in Washington; a clarification of views showing complete differences of opinion between Israel and its one possible friend among the Communist countries. Why he is so delighted with this formula is hard to understand — it means that Israel stands alone in a hostile world.'

Israel's military might
'The result of Begin insisting on Israel going headlong down a lonely road must be another armed conflict. Many Israelis seem to cherish the idea of a war of revenge for the Yom Kippur War, just as the French wanted "revanche" after the Franco-Prussian War of 1870. Certainly Israel has the armed might to inflict a crushing defeat on the Arabs, if she gets in her blows first, and if she is allowed to wage such a war by the Americans and Russians. This was confirmed by the International Institute for Strategic Studies in September 1977. But the "ifs" are so formidable that they make the whole idea of Israel going to war seem nonsensical. Dayan's declaration in Brussels on the 15th of September 1977, on his way to meet President Carter, that "... It is preferable to oppose the establishment of a Palestinian State and risk war now instead of accepting such a State and risk war in ten years in much worse security conditions," must worry every Jew, and all friends of Israel.

'Would Russia stand by and see the Arabs overwhelmed as they were in 1967? If such a war was waged in defiance of the Americans, would they risk an atomic confrontation with the Russians to protect Israel from a Soviet counter-attack? Finally, even if Israel got away with another war, what would she achieve? The "liberation" of Damascus, Cairo and Amman? The expulsion of the Arabs from the West Bank and the Gaza Strip?

'All the Arabs I know tell me that they have learned their lessons, and will never become refugees again, will never move voluntarily. Will they be driven out by force? Such a concept is not only impractical, it is also highly immoral — it is unthinkable that Jews of all people, the victims of centuries of oppression, should even contemplate so horrifying a thought!

The De Gaulle precedent
'The whole idea of Israel going ahead without America is so absurd that there is one ray of hope — Begin's common sense may overcome his mighty declarations, his clichés of thought and speech, his proclaimed principles and ideology.

'There is a precedent. General Charles de Gaulle had declared that Algeria was an inalienable part of France which could never be surrendered. It was to put this programme into effect that he became President of France once more. Later, his representatives sat at Evian with "terrorists" and other representatives of the Algerian Liberation Front. And he duly granted Algeria independence — and carried the vast majority of the French people with him.

'Begin has done some things which indicate that he is not as stiff-necked as his speeches make him out to be. There is the appointment of Moshe Dayan as Foreign Minister. Dayan certainly does not hold any deep convictions about Israel being obliged for mystic religious reasons to retain the West Bank and Gaza. His approach to problems is entirely pragmatic, he is not fettered by principles or by what he said yesterday. When Dayan's approach is borne in mind, Begin's appointment of him seems completely inconsistent with his proclaimed determination to hold the occupied areas.

'So I pray that Begin will emulate de Gaulle, and will amaze the world by becoming the first Israeli leader to grant the Palestinians the rights of self-determination and to exist as an independent people. Strangely enough, he is better able to adopt such a policy than any of his opponents ever were. If he does, he will deserve the eternal gratitude of the Jewish people, and will rank among the great leaders of history!'

EPILOGUE

CO-EXISTENCE IN SEPARATE STATES

The last discussion I had with Eliachar about this book was in September, 1977, during the period of the Jewish New Year. This is a time when Jews review their lives, examine what moral progress they have made, engage in critical self-judgments, compile their spiritual accounts. It is also a custom for Israel's leaders to sum up the state of the nation.

Many Israelis claimed that the position looked better than it had for years. The disengagement agreements with Egypt and Syria were working satisfactorily; there had been no shooting on the borders with these two countries for many months. The Lebanese bloodbath was proving that the Arabs were completely disunited. The P.L.O. had turned down President Carter's suggestion that they accept Security Council Resolution 242, so as to justify their inclusion in the negotiating process. Menahem Begin was becoming a "father figure" in Israel, providing the appearance of a strong government in place of the weak and divided one of Yitzhak Rabin.

Elie Eliachar was not impressed by all these arguments of the optimists.

'True', he said, 'Begin is providing strong leadership — but he is leading the nation in the wrong direction. The failure of President Carter's efforts to get the P.L.O. to accept Resolution 242 has brought the danger of war appreciably nearer. It is hard to see what course of action President Carter can now take — or, for that matter, what Begin and Sadat and Assad and Hussein can do.

'It horrifies me that some Israelis seem to be pleased about the tragic blood-bath in Lebanon. I don't suggest that they are delighted that some 60,000 people have been killed, and many more wounded, only that they think the tragedy proves their hawkish arguments that the Arabs are impossible people with whom to deal. Thus Shimon Peres, our former Minister of Defence, described the Lebanese civil war as a boon for our future, and said that "the Arab leaders had gone on safari, so that there is nobody available with whom we can talk peace, even when we want to do so." I think these views are specious, and are liable to boomerang.

'Reliance on inter-Arab divisions is one of the most dangerous of all our delusions; time and again we have found to our cost that these disappear suddenly, and we face a united Arab world in war. This happened both in 1967 and 1973. Our great, over-riding need is not inter-Arab tension, but an end to Arab-Jewish tension. All wars have a tendency to spread out beyond frontiers; nothing is harder to contain than bloodshed. Our hope lies in peace and cooperation in the Middle East, not in internecine Arab quarrels. Although they may disagree about everything else, on one thing all Arabs agree: the problem of the Palestinians must be solved and the occupied territories surrendered.

'Begin makes great play of the statement in the P.L.O. Covenant that Israel cannot continue to exist as a state in the Middle East, and must be replaced by a secular, democratic state dominated by the Palestinians. He compares this document frequently to Hitler's "Mein Kampf." The inference is that whoever recommends that Israelis should talk to the members of the P.L.O. is urging Jews to cooperate in their own destruction while the world looks on, to go like lambs to the slaughter.

'This is sheer sophistry. The Jews destroyed by Hitler had no power to resist, while Israel must always be strong enough to deter any Arab attack. It is on what people do, not what they say, that they must be judged. Otherwise, the Palestinians can quote Begin, Arik Sharon and others to say that there is no point in talking to the Israelis, because they have said over and over again that they will never accept the fact of the Palestinian entity. If Begin really means that there should be negotiations without any pre-conditions, whatever is stated in the P.L.O. Covenant is completely irrelevant. The Covenant of the P.L.O. can also be discussed.

The Arab attitude
'Throughout my discussions with you I have emphasized the mistakes that the Zionist leadership made and are still making. But their errors are trifling compared to those made by the Palestinian leaders. They refused to cooperate with the Jews in the revival of the land they shared. In 1936 they rejected the partition proposed by the Royal Commission headed by Lord Peel, which the Jews accepted. In 1947, they turned down the partition approved by the U.N. Time and time again they have tried to destroy the Jews, first of Palestine and then of Israel, by force of arms.

'This dream that they can exterminate Israel is a dangerous delusion of a minority of Palestinians: the overwhelming majority, particularly those living on the West Bank and in the Gaza Strip, know that Israel is here to stay. The trouble is that the Palestinian leaders fall in love with words; so, for that matter, do our present leaders.

'They must face it that we are here to stay; we must face it that the Arabs in the areas are also here to stay, as are the Arabs in Galilee and other parts of Israel. The alternative is mutual destruction.

'The only hope for Israelis and Palestinians alike is that they should co-exist in two separate sovereign secure states. This truth has been self-evident, although obscured, for numerous decades. It is now so clear that almost everybody in the world, except some Palestinians and some Israelis, now accept it as the only possible solution to the problem of the Middle East, a problem that may destroy our area and obliterate part of the world if it is allowed to remain unsolved.

'The trouble is that the Israelis set up a stereotype of the Palestinian — they visualize a terrorist, armed to the teeth, determined to kill every Jewish man, woman and child — then say, "Look at this monster — nobody can expect us to talk to him!" But the Palestinians do not all fit the stereotype, very few of them do. Most of them are sensible, reasonable men, longing for peace and an end to the tension, although they have been deeply hurt in their national pride. If we come forward with proposals to help them to establish their own state, they will respond eagerly and will cooperate with us. So I think. Even if I am wrong, we have no alternative.

'We must try to find a peaceful solution, even one that involves risks. We take incredible risks in war — peace demands equal courage. A bold approach, combined with vigilance, could bring us the greatest of victories, Peace.

'Recently, "El Fajar", an extremist Arab daily, published a special issue in which I and other members of the Israeli Council for Peace with the Palestinians expressed our views. These may seem very liberal to some Israeli Jews, but to Palestinian extremists they are far in the other direction. Yet the editors of "El Fajar" provided us with a platform. This was the first time that such a thing had happened in years.'

His views have made him unpopular with many Israelis. Sometimes the criticism has been virulent. He is now in his late seventies. Has not the time come for him to forsake the heat and dust of the battle, to allow younger champions to fight for the causes he holds so dear?

'As long as I believe that I can contribute something to getting justice for the Palestinians, and Peace and Unity for Israel, I will fight on and on and on, whatever the consequences. I feel that I have little time to get my message across, so I am now working a 14-hour day to do so.'

Despite all his efforts, his writings, speeches, meetings, travels and contacts, he still expresses the views of a minority in Israel. Does he think that he is making headway?

'A Jew must be an optimist to survive. I am convinced that ultimately the truth will prevail. So of course I believe we are making progress.

'I can sum up my attitude by quoting to you two poems. One is by Judah Halevi, the greatest Jewish poet. He wrote in the twelfth century, "I am in the West, but my heart is in the uttermost East." In the twentieth century, his successors are living in the East, in Israel, in Asia, but in their hearts they yearn to be in the West. I want Israel to integrate into the East, without giving up any Jewish culture or the best that the West can offer. Then everything will fall into place, and our problems will be solved.

'The other poem is by William Blake, who wrote, "I will not cease from mental fight, nor shall my sword sleep in my hand, till we have built Jerusalem in England's green and pleasant land." I will never stop my fight till we have built the Jerusalem of our dreams 'in the green and pleasant and peaceful fields of the Middle East."

POSTSCRIPT: JANUARY, 1978

AFTER PRESIDENT SADAT'S VISIT TO JERUSALEM

An Israel edition of this book was first published in September, 1977: by the time a second edition for England was printed, only three months later, the face of the Middle East had been transformed by President Anwar Sadat's offer to go to Jerusalem to address the Knesset, and Prime Minister Menahem Begin's immediate and imaginative acceptance. From then on, events moved at headlong speed.

Eliachar was in London in November and December, and, incidentally, he had long talks there with two moderate members of the Palestine Liberation Organisation. He and I had a final discussion late in December, 1977.

'The daring and brilliance of President Sadat, and the vision and courage of Mr. Begin, achieved in one stroke what I had dreamt about for decades — real peoce negotiations,' said Eliachar. 'All those years I had preached that Israelis should stop looking at the Arabs as stereotypes — and, equally, that the Arabs should not see the Israelis as stereotypes — but I could never break through the excessive caution and fear of going out on a limb exhibited by every Israeli leader since Ben-Gurion left politics. In one month, Sadat and Begin proved that they were not trapped by their prior declarations. It is clear that both of them, perhaps because they feel time pressing on their backs, want to enter history as the great peacemakers. The reaction of the Israeli and Egyptian peoples proved that it is nonsense to talk of nations hating each other: everyone wants peace and hates war.

'You will remember that I said that Begin might prove to be Israel's General de Gaulle. Just as de Gaulle was elected to keep Algeria French, and then gave it independence, so I hoped that Begin, elected on an annexationist platform, would choose instead an imaginative solution to the Middle East problem at odds with that platform. He has more than justified my somewhat paradoxical hopes. By his response to President Sadat's unprecedented challenge, he has shown more courage than any Israeli premier since David Ben-Gurion.'

Does this mean that peace is around the corner?

'In his masterly address to the Knesset and his subsequent speeches and press conferences, President Sadat has accepted Israel as a full partner in the Middle East complex of nations, and has recognised her right to exist in absolute security in agreed and guaranteed borders. In return, he expects Israel to surrender all territories occupied in 1967, and to grant the Palestinians the right to self-determination in their own homeland. He has called on all Arabs to follow his lead. As you know, with slight modifications, I believe that there is a moral duty on Jews to accept these principles.

'A great change has become apparent in Begin's attitude. He has dropped the mystic line that we are enjoined by the Almighty to retain sovereignty over the occupied areas, which he calls Judaea and Samaria. The new philosophy is called a functional one, and the stress is on security, not mysticism. Of course, I don't think any reputable Arab leader will accept any plan that doesn't guarantee the Palestinians full self-determination, just as no Israeli will accept a plan that does not guarantee Israel full security.'

What about the rejection front, headed by Libya and Iraq, and supported to the full by the P.L.O.? Will they succeed in reguting the new peace drive?

'In London I met unofficially with official moderate members of the P.L.O. and their British supporters. I said to them bluntly that it was absurd for the P.L.O. to go on and on and on with their line that Israel as such must be destroyed, that it should be replaced by a secular democratic state. And I warned the P.L.O. that they were missing their historic opportunity, created for all the Palestinians by the courage and wisdom of President Sadat, an opportunity that might never recur for them. I said that their attitude was as irrational as that of the Gush Emunim fanatics, who swore that they would never surrender an inch of the West Bank, and would never allow a Palestinian State to be created.

'Much to my surprise, they agreed with me in principle, subject to certain modifications. But they could not see their way clear to influencing the main leadership of their Organisation, because of Israel's inflexible attitude towards the P.L.O. They said to me, "Israelis insist that we must repudiate the clause in our Covenant calling for the abolition of Israel, before they will agree to talk with us, and add that in any case they cannot deal with us because our hands are red with Jewish blood. Why didn't they insist on President Sadat revoking the first clause of the Constitution of his party, which adopted the no's of Khartoum? Instead, he was welcomed as a hero in Jerusalem. If Israel would only open the door a chink, we moderates in the P.L.O. would get a chance."

'They kept emphasising that it was Israel that made conditions, impossible for the moderates. They insist that any peace that does not embrace not only the Palestinians living in the West Bank and the Gaza Strip, but the hundreds of thousands outside it, cannot endure. This means bringing the P.L.O. into the negotiating process. I am inclined to agree with them that we cannot leave a running sore open — provided they agreed to President Sadat's welcoming Israel as one of the peoples of the Middle East.

'I repeat my formula for peace: guarantees of security for Israel within her 1967 borders, subject to minor modifications; self-determination for the Palestinians in their own homeland in the West Bank and Gaza Strip; demilitarization of that state for some years to come; a condominium or borough system for Jerusalem.

'We are living through a phase more hopeful — and, at the same time, more critical — than any we have known since 1947. As King Hassan II of Morocco said, in the presence of President Sadat, "Peace between Israel and the Arabs will bring about the same kind of fruitful collaboration as existed in the Jewish Golden Era, one of the richest epochs in the histories of two great peoples, both descendants of the patriarch Abraham. Not only the Middle East, but the world as a whole, will benefit." On the other hand, if — God forbid — President Sadat's initiative fails, the armed conflict that will inevitably follow may involve the whole world in chaos.

'As a Jew, an Israeli and a devoted Zionist, I believe

that the *raison d'être* of Israel as an Independent State is its Jewishness, i.e. that Jews shall always be the majority within its borders. If the Palestinian Arab population now living in the West Bank and Gaza is attached to Israel, they will be the majority towards the end of this century, Jewish immigration notwithstanding. Add to this factor that the Israeli Arabs are and shall remain closely attached to their brethren, and you have no difficulty in realizing that such a demographic development may undermine Israel's viability and endanger her survival.

'If Begin and his government give the Nation the inspired and imaginative leadership that the great opportunity given to Israel requires, we can achieve those blessings of peace, so wonderfully described by the prophet Isaiah, to which you refer on page 14 of this book. And I will be able to recite the Prayer of Thanks to the Almighty that I have been allowed to live to see that day.'

THE END

ACKNOWLEDGMENTS OF PICTURES

The pictures used in this book were provided by the Jewish Agency Archives, the Jerusalem Municipality's archives, the Israel Government Press Office, Elie Eliachar and Gaalya Cornfeld.

PHILIP GILLON, a veteran Israeli journalist, has been for many years one of the main feature writers of "The Jerusalem Post," and writer of a weekly column on television.

Born in Johannesburg, South Africa, he practised as a lawyer in that city for several years. Members of his family were among the most prominent Zionists in South Africa, and, as soon as the State was proclaimed, he immigrated to Israel. For two years he was a member of a kibbutz, Kevutzat Schiller.

After leaving the kibbutz, he became one of the founders of a new town in the south of Israel, Ashkelon, where he served as city manager. Subsequently, he became the correspondent for the southern region of Israel for "The Jerusalem Post" and "Maariv."

Moving to Jerusalem in 1960, he joined the editorial staff of "The Jerusalem Post," where he has worked ever since. He is also the Jerusalem correspondent of "The Montreal Star," of Canada, and of the Argus group, of South Africa.

His novel about South Africa, "Frail Barrier," was published by Vangaurd Press in the U.S.A., and by Hutchinson in England. Together with his wife, Hadassah Gillon, he edited a book on "Science Education in Developing Countries," based on one of the Rehovot Conferences, which was published by Praeger in the U.S.A. Recently he edited "Kibbutz + Bauhaus — an architect's way in a new land," the biography of architect Arieh Sharon. He and his wife are now working on a book on "Science in Israel" for Keter Press, Jerusalem.

LIBRARY OF DAVIDSON COLLEGE